GREEKS & ROMANS

GALORE PARK

GREEKS&ROMANS

A M Wright

www.galorepark.co.uk

Published by Galore Park Publishing Ltd
19/21 Sayers Lane, Tenterden, Kent TN30 6BW
www.galorepark.co.uk

Text copyright © A M Wright 2010

Layout by Qué
Technical illustrations by Simon Tegg and Ian Moores
Cartoon illustrations by Rosie Forster

Printed by Replika Press, India

ISBN: 978 1 905735 43 3

First published 2011, reprinted 2011

Details of other Galore Park publications are available at www.galorepark.co.uk

ISEB Revision Guides, publications and examination papers may also be obtained from Galore Park

The following photographs are used by permission of the agencies indicated:
Page 4 Brian Jannsen/Alamy, p.9 Ancient Art and Architecture Collection Ltd/The Bridgeman Art Library Nationality, p.12 Prisma Archivo/Alamy, p.17 akg-images/Erich Lessing, p.20 Louvre, Paris, France/The Bridgeman Art Library, p.23 Marion Kaplan/Alamy, p.27 akg-images/Nimatallah, p.32 World History Archive/Alamy, p.35 akg-images/Erich Lessing, p.40 maurice joseph/Alamy, p.42 The Art Gallery Collection/Alamy, p.43 The Art Gallery Collection/Alamy, p.50 akg-images/Peter Connolly, p.51 akg-images/Erich Lessing, p.52 akg-images/Peter Connolly, p.53 The Print Collector/Alamy, p.54 Angus McBride Gladiators © Osprey Publishing (www.ospreypublishing.com), p.57 akg-images/Peter Connolly, p.58 akg-images/Peter Connolly, p.60 Robert Harding Picture Library Ltd/Alamy, p.67 The Print Collector/Alamy, p.68 akg-images/Erich Lessing, p.70 Domenico Tondini/Alamy, p.72 akg-images/Peter Connolly, p.73 Robert Harding Picture Library Ltd/Alamy, p.74 Art Kowalsky/Alamy, p.79 Sotheby's/akg-images, p.81 The Art Gallery Collection/Alamy, p.83 World History Archive/Alamy, p.88 Jeff Morgan 16/Alamy, p.91 Angus McBride Roman Legionary 58 BC–AD 69 © Osprey Publishing, p.93 Brian Delf Greek and Roman Artillery 399 BC–AD 363 © Osprey Publishing, p.94 Richard Bonson © Dorling Kindersley, p.96 akg-images/Erich Lessing, p.102 N R R Oulton, p.103 Skyscan Photolibrary/Alamy, p.105 Brian Harris/Alamy, p.109 By permission of Sussex Archaeological Society, p.111 Robert Estall photo agency/Alamy, p.112 By permission of the British Museum and the Centre for the Study of Ancient Documents, University of Oxford.

ABOUT THE AUTHOR

After spells in London and Oxford, A M Wright is currently teaching at St. Mary's, Ascot. She studied at the University of St Andrews and Corpus Christi College, Oxford. She has served on the Councils of the Joint Association of Classical Teachers and the Society for the Promotion of Hellenic Studies. She has written Latin Prep Workbooks 1A and 1B (published by Galore Park) as well as a 5-volume series on *Inside Ancient Greece.*

In her spare time, she reads voraciously, enjoys art and plays the 'cello in her local orchestra. She also enjoys playing the piano and clarinet.

Dedication

felibus optimis - B. et B.

INTRODUCTION

About this book

This book provides an introduction to what life was really like for the Romans as they carried out their daily routine in Rome, in Britain and in the army. Romans also loved myths and legends, and some of the most exciting and famous classical myths are covered in the following pages.

You may have chosen to read this book for interest or it may be part of your school work. If you are using this book for Common Entrance study, you will find that it provides you with everything you need to know for the culture section of your Common Entrance examination. There are four main sections to this book – Greek Mythology, The City of Rome, Domestic Life, and the Roman Army and Roman Britain. Your teacher may want you to learn particular sections, rather than the whole book, but it is still worth reading every section to improve your understanding of the cultural background to the Roman world. To assist you with preparation, exam-style practice questions are included.

Questions

In the Common Entrance exam you will have a choice of questions (two per section). Each question is divided into two parts. The first part looks for a **detailed** description of, for example, the organisation of the Roman army. Here, accurate detail is your key to getting good marks. *Learn* the information thoroughly and *apply* it accurately. Avoid irrelevant information that is not connected to the question (for example, don't write about marriage ceremonies if you are asked about coming-of-age ceremonies).

The second part of the question is your **personal response** to the information or story about which you have written. It is important to give a meaningful response to the second part of the question and, where possible, to back up your answer with reference to what you wrote in the first part. For example, if asked why the Romans might tell the story of Scaevola to their children, don't just say, 'because he was brave'. Explain that Romans would want their children to be as brave on behalf of their fatherland as Scaevola was and that, for the Romans, risking one's life to save one's country was a very important civic virtue.

In Common Entrance, eight marks are generally given for the first part of the question, and two marks for the second part. Teachers may choose to allocate marks differently.

There are plenty of questions here for you to try. You may not wish to attempt them all at once. Choose one or two, then, as you become more familiar with the stories and facts, try some of the harder ones.

Some extension questions (including suggestions for research and project work) are also included. This type of question will not be asked in Common Entrance, but answering these questions will help you to think more deeply about the subject and to widen your knowledge.

Exam revision

There isn't really much excuse for not knowing the culture section for your exam. It's in English, the information and stories are interesting and all you have to do is learn the information and apply it in a clear, coherent way to the questions you are asked. Whichever sections you are learning, certain points apply throughout:

- Know how to **spell the names**. Nothing is more irritating for an examiner than reading about 'Romeullus and Reems' or 'Hurcules'.

- **Think about the question**. If you are asked to discuss how slaves were treated and how they might gain their freedom, you are *not* expected to write about how they came to be slaves in the first place.

- **Check which story** you are writing about. If you are asked to tell the story of Perseus, you won't get marks for writing about the killing of the Minotaur – that was Theseus!

An excellent book to help you with revision is *Study Skills* by Elizabeth Holtom (ISBN 9781902984599 published by Galore Park www.galorepark.co.uk).

A M Wright
January 2011

GREEKS

ROMANS

CHAPTER 1 PERSEUS, JASON AND THESEUS

1.1 The story of Perseus

The birth of Perseus

Perseus was one of the greatest Greek heroes of all time, and yet he was lucky to have been born. Perseus's grandfather King Acrisius had been warned by an oracle that he would die at the hands of his grandson. Naturally, Acrisius, who was the king of Argos, did not wish to die, so he locked his only child, Danae, in a great tower made of bronze and forbade her to have any contact with the outside world, believing that this would prevent her from ever having a baby. However, Fate cannot be avoided and when Zeus, the ruler of the gods, heard about poor, lonely Danae he took pity on her and visited her, disguised as a shower of gold.

Nine months later, Danae gave birth to a beautiful baby boy, whom she called Perseus. When the terrified guards reported the news to Acrisius, he fell into a violent rage. Bursting into the tower, he threatened to kill Danae there and then. However, Acrisius did not want to be directly responsible for killing his daughter, so he ordered his slaves to put her and the baby into a large wooden chest, and hurl it into the sea.

Danae wept as the chest was nailed up, fully expecting to drown in the merciless sea. However, the gods took pity on the sobbing girl and the chest did not sink, but floated on the waves until it came to the island of Seriphos. Here it was found by a fisherman named Dictys, who was mending his nets on the shore. Opening it, he was astounded to discover a beautiful girl with a baby nestling in her arms. Dictys was a kind man and he took the girl back to his home and gave her shelter.

Over the years, Perseus grew up to be a fine, handsome boy and Danae kept her good looks. One day Dictys's cruel brother, Polydectes, the king of Seriphos, caught sight of Danae and fell in love with her. He constantly asked Danae to marry him, but Danae did not trust Polydectes and Perseus loathed him. The king returned Perseus's hatred and plotted to get rid of him; for Polydectes mistakenly believed that Danae would accept him if she no longer had a son.

The plot

Polydectes knew that, if Perseus 'disappeared', Danae would assume the king had murdered him. Therefore, Polydectes came up with a cunning plan. First, he pretended that he was going to marry another woman. Then he asked all the young men of Seriphos to provide him with a wedding gift of one fine horse. Now, although Perseus was handsome, brave and wise, he was poor and had no horses, nor any money to buy one. At the engagement party the other young men mocked Perseus for not bringing a gift, so he proclaimed that he would bring Polydectes whatever the king wanted. With an evil grin, Polydectes replied that he would ask Perseus for just one item – the head of the Gorgon Medusa.

The assembled company fell silent, for the Gorgon Medusa was a terrible monster with snakes for hair, whose glance turned men into stone. Perseus knew that Polydectes had trapped him, but he was determined to tackle his mission. If he refused the challenge, he would be shown up as a coward and he would be unable to protect his mother. Happily, the gods, who had saved Perseus once, now came to his aid again. Hermes, the messenger of the gods, gave him a sharp sickle to cut off Medusa's head and Athene, the grey-eyed goddess of wisdom, lent him her shining shield.

This famous bronze sculpture of Perseus with the head of Medusa is by the 16th century artist Benvenuto Cellini

Athene also advised Perseus that three old women called the Graeae could tell him where Medusa lived. The Graeae were ugly old hags who, between the three of them, had just one eye and one tooth, which they would pass from one to the other. Perseus slipped up behind them and grabbed the eye as it was being passed from one crone to another. Perseus refused to return the eye until they told him where the Gorgon lived and where he might find Hades's helmet of darkness and a pair of winged sandals. Spitting with anger, the Graeae revealed the necessary information. Perseus collected his final pieces of equipment from the Underworld, then flew off on his winged sandals, ready to tackle Medusa.

Triumph!

The helmet of darkness made its wearer invisible, so Perseus was able to approach Medusa unseen. Even though the monster was asleep, Perseus dared not look at the Gorgon directly. Instead, he used Athene's highly polished shield as a mirror to watch Medusa's every movement as he crept closer and closer. Finally, he was near enough to attack! Snatching his sickle, and still looking only at the reflection in the mirror, he lopped off the Gorgon's head. Then he grasped it by its snake-infested hair and thrust it into his bag. Medusa's sisters tried to come to her aid, but Perseus flew off into the sky on his winged sandals. Looking backwards, he was astonished to see a winged horse, Pegasus, springing fully-formed out of Medusa's dead body.

On the way home, Perseus caught sight of a beautiful girl called Andromeda, tied to a cliff-face. Weeping pitifully, she told him: 'My parents boasted of my beauty and the gods sent a sea monster to ravage our land to teach them a lesson. Now an oracle has decreed that I must be sacrificed to the sea monster, or our country will never be free from it.'

Perseus was determined to save the beautiful girl. First, he persuaded Andromeda's parents to let him marry her if he killed the sea monster, and then he tackled the hideous beast as it swam towards her. Swooping down from high above, he stabbed it in the neck and watched it sink back lifeless into the waves. Perseus claimed Andromeda's hand in marriage and, stopping only to turn her uncle, Phineus, into stone when he tried to interfere, he continued back to Seriphos.

When Perseus arrived home, he found Polydectes dining with his companions. Perseus entered the palace, carrying the bag with Medusa's head and exclaimed, 'See how I have carried out my task!' As they turned to look at him, he drew the head of the Gorgon out of the bag and turned them all into stone. Thus Perseus saved his mother. He made Dictys king of Seriphos in place of Polydectes, before leaving to look for his grandfather Acrisius. However, the dire warning of the oracle was to come true after all. For, on the way to Argos, Perseus stopped to take part in an athletics contest. Entering the discus competition, he let fly a discus with a mighty swing of his arm. Far into the air flew the discus until it dropped, striking an old man in the crowd of onlookers, killing him stone dead. The old man was none other than King Acrisius.

1.2 Jason and the Golden Fleece

Jason's early life

Another mighty hero was Jason, the son of Aeson, King of Iolcos. When Jason was a young boy, his wicked uncle, Pelias, seized the throne from Aeson. Aeson fled into exile, and sent his little son away into the care of the centaur Chiron. Like all centaurs, Chiron had the upper torso of a man and the lower body of a horse, but he was also noted for his wisdom and he brought Jason up to be a noble young man. Jason was always determined to regain his position as the rightful ruler of Iolcos and, when he was old enough, he set off to deal with Pelias.

The return to Iolcos

As Jason approached Iolcos, a frail old woman asked him to help her across a deep stream. Jason had good manners and agreed at once. Lifting up the woman, he set out into the water. However, the woman was surprisingly heavy and Jason nearly fell over. He recovered and reached the other side safely, but he lost one sandal to the current. As Jason set the old woman down, he was shocked to see her suddenly transformed into a beautiful

goddess, Hera, the wife of Zeus. 'You have passed my test,' she announced, 'for you treated me with courtesy when I appeared to be a poor old woman. If you ever need my help, I shall grant it.' Then she vanished back into the heavens.

Jason was both pleased and surprised, and continued on to Iolcos. When Jason entered the palace, Pelias immediately realised who this stranger was, for an oracle had warned Pelias to beware of a man who wore only one sandal. Forewarned, Pelias had time to prepare himself for the meeting with his long-lost nephew. When Jason announced who he was, Pelias pretended to be delighted to see him and promised that he would hand over power. Then he proclaimed a great feast to celebrate Jason's return.

At the feast, Pelias ordered a bard (or folk singer) to sing of the Golden Fleece. This Fleece was a sheepskin made of gold which belonged to King Aeetes of Colchis. Aeetes was determined that no one would steal his Fleece and had set a fierce dragon which never slept to guard it. Jason listened eagerly to the bard, fascinated by the story. After the song ended, Pelias lamented that young men nowadays were too weak and too cowardly to attempt such a great quest. Jason fell straight into Pelias's trap. 'You are wrong, Uncle,' he boasted. 'I am not afraid of the dragon. I shall fetch the Fleece!'

The quest for the fleece

Colchis was situated near the Black Sea, a long way from Iolcos. Jason knew that he needed companions to help him on his venture, so he sent out an invitation to all the important warriors, offering them the chance to win great fame. Many of those who chose to sail with him had also been educated by Chiron, and his crew included Heracles, Orpheus, Castor and Pollux. The gods gave Jason magic wood to build his ship, which was called the *Argo*, and the crew became known as the Argonauts (sailors of the *Argo*).

6

The Argonauts faced many adventures on the way to Colchis, including sailing through the Clashing Rocks and defeating the dreadful Harpies. These birds had the faces of women and snatched food greedily from men's mouths. At last the Argonauts reached Colchis, where King Aeetes greeted them warmly. However, when he learned that Jason had come to take the Golden Fleece, he was incensed. 'The Fleece is mine,' he hissed. 'But you may have it if you carry out four tasks in a single day. You must tame two wild bulls – their horns and hooves are made of brass and they breathe flames, so you may die in the attempt! If you overcome the bulls, you must yoke them to a stone plough and use it to plough an uncultivated field. Next, you must sow the special seed from this bag.' The king sniggered evilly as he handed the seed to Jason. 'Then you must overcome the dragon which guards the Golden Fleece. A hero like you should have no difficulty doing these things.'

Jason retired from the king in despair, knowing that he was unprepared for such deeds. However, the king's daughter, Medea, followed him. Medea had fallen madly in love with Jason and offered to betray her father, if Jason would marry her and take her away from Colchis. Jason agreed to her terms. Then Medea explained her plan.

'I am a witch, skilled in the ways of sorcery. You will succeed only by using my magic arts. First, you must smear this ointment all over your body – it will protect you from the bulls' fiery breath. Second, those are no ordinary seeds in the bag. You have been given the teeth of a dragon. When you sow them, hundreds of warriors will spring up from the soil fully-armed. You cannot fight them all yourself; you must make them fight each other. Therefore, throw a stone into their midst; they will think that they are being  attacked from behind and will kill each other. Finally, here is a potion to send the dragon to sleep while you snatch the Fleece.'

The next day, everything went as planned. Jason accomplished all the tasks and sailed away with the Fleece. Medea went with him, bringing her younger brother, Apsyrtus. Aeetes was furious and sailed after them. Then Medea revealed her ruthless streak: seizing her little brother, she killed him and cut his body into pieces which she then scattered on the waves. Aeetes was distraught and, as he stopped to collect the gory remains of his son's body, the Argonauts escaped.

When Jason returned to Iolcos, Medea tricked Pelias's daughters into killing their father. Jason took control of the country and settled down to rule it. However, he eventually moved to Corinth where he grew tired of Medea and abandoned her. Jason may have forgotten Medea's vengeful nature, but he was soon reminded of her capacity for ruthlessness. Desperate to hurt Jason for abandoning her, Medea killed their two children and escaped to Athens in a chariot drawn by dragons. Jason died a lonely old man.

1.3 Theseus and the Minotaur

Theseus's early life

Another of the great Greek heroes was Theseus, the son of King Aegeus of Athens and Princess Aethra of Troezen. Before Theseus was born, Aegeus left Troezen to return to Athens. As Aegeus departed, he said to Aethra: 'If our child is a boy, bring him up to be brave. I have placed something for him under this large boulder. When he is old enough and strong enough to lift the boulder, send him to Athens where I shall look after him.'

As Theseus grew up, he repeatedly tried to lift the boulder. Finally, he was successful and under the rock he found a pair of sandals and a fine sword. Delighted, he raced back to his mother and told her that he was setting out to Athens to find his father. Aethra wept, fearing that she would never see her son again.

On the way to Athens, Theseus met with and overcame many dangers. He killed Periphetes, the club-bearer, and took his club for his own use. Next he overcame Sinis, who killed unlucky travellers by tying them to two bent pine trees and then letting the trees loose. His victims died horribly, ripped in two. Theseus tied Sinis to the two trees and sent him to his death. Now it was the turn of Sciron, who ordered passers-by to bend down to wash his feet before kicking them off the narrow cliff path where he lurked. Theseus showed him no mercy and soon Sciron's body was whirling through the air down onto the sharp rocks beneath. Theseus also executed Procrustes, an evil man who offered hospitality to tired travellers but whose bed was always the wrong size for his unwary guests. Those who were too short for the bed Procrustes offered them were stretched on a rack, and those who were too tall had their limbs hacked off. Theseus rid the world of Procrustes by treating him in the same manner.

Finally, Theseus arrived at Athens and made his way to the palace, intending to find his father. However, Aegeus was now married to the cunning witch Medea, who had been abandoned by Jason. She realised who Theseus was and feared that he would gain power in Athens in place of her son. She offered Theseus a goblet of wine containing poison. Theseus was just raising the glass to drain the wine when Aegeus recognised the sword that Theseus was carrying. Knocking the poisoned wine to the ground, Aegeus embraced his long lost son, and the wicked Medea was driven from the palace.

The deadly tribute

Despite the rejoicing at Theseus's arrival, it soon became clear that there was great sorrow within the Athenian court. Eventually, Aegeus explained that it was time for seven youths and seven maidens to be sent to Crete to feed the hungry Minotaur. The Minotaur was a terrible creature, half man, half bull, which lived in the Labyrinth, an underground maze which the Greek inventor Daedalus had built beneath the palace of King Minos on the island of Crete. Year after year, seven Athenian maidens and seven Athenian young men were sent to Crete to be fed to the Minotaur. King Minos of Crete demanded this deadly annual tribute from the Athenians because they had killed one of his sons in war. Minos was a great king, but it was his fault that the Minotaur had been born. Minos had broken a promise to sacrifice a fine bull to Poseidon and the sea god was so angry that he devised a

This Roman mosaic shows Theseus tackling the Minotaur

terrible revenge. He sent Minos's wife, Pasiphae, mad and she fell passionately in love with a bull and gave birth to the Minotaur. The presence of this monster was a constant reminder of Pasiphae's strange love, but Minos dared not kill the beast. Instead, he hid his shameful secret underground in the Labyrinth, away from human eyes.

Theseus at once volunteered to go in place of one of the youths. Aegeus begged his son not to risk so terrible a death, but Theseus responded bravely: 'If I am not prepared to risk my life to save my country, then I am not worthy to be its prince.' Reluctantly, Aegeus agreed, but asked Theseus for one favour: 'The ship sailing to Crete always carries black sails as a sign of mourning. If you return alive from Crete, change the sails to white so that I shall know that you are safe.' Theseus promised that he would do so. Then he embraced his father and departed, accompanied by the other weeping victims.

Theseus in Crete

When the ship arrived at Crete, the doomed Athenians disembarked. The king's daughter Ariadne was watching their arrival impassively, but when she caught sight of handsome Theseus she immediately fell in love with him. Desperate to prevent so noble a man from being killed by the Minotaur, she made her way by night to the prison where the Athenians were held and gave Theseus some magic thread and a sword.

The next day, Theseus and the other captives were thrust into the Labyrinth and the gate crashed shut behind them. However, Theseus was not afraid. Ordering the others to wait at the entrance, he tied the thread to the gate and, paying it out as he walked, he set off into the heart of the maze. Soon he tracked down the dreaded Minotaur and attacked it. When the beast lay dead on the ground, Theseus followed the string back to the entrance, where his terrified companions still waited. After reassuring them that he had despatched the Minotaur, Theseus led them towards the harbour where their boat – and Ariadne – were waiting. Then they slipped away unseen.

Theseus had promised Ariadne that he would take her back to Athens and marry her, but when the Athenians reached the island of Naxos, Theseus callously abandoned her. Although she was eventually rescued by the god Dionysos, who fell in love with her, the other gods were angry with Theseus's betrayal. Some Greeks believed that the gods made Theseus forget to change the sails of his ship. Whether or not this was true, the ship did indeed sail home with its black sails aloft. The result was dire. Every day since Theseus's departure, King Aegeus had remained on top of a high cliff, hoping to catch sight of his ship returning from Crete. When he saw that it carried black sails, he assumed the worst. Grief stricken, he cried out, 'Theseus, my son, is dead!' and hurled himself off the cliff to drown in the lashing waves beneath.

Since then, the sea has been called the Aegean Sea to commemorate Aegeus's tragic end.

Exercise 1.1

1. (a) Tell the story of what happened to Danae.
   (b) Was Acrisius correct to deal with Danae and her son as he did? Why?
2. (a) Tell the story of Perseus and the Gorgon.
   (b) Of the gifts which the gods gave Perseus, which do you think was the most useful and why?
3. (a) Tell the story of Perseus's adventures on his return from having killed Medusa.
   (b) Do you think that Polydectes deserved his fate? Give reasons for your answer.

Extension work

Draw EITHER Perseus dealing with the Graeae OR a detailed picture of Perseus slaying Medusa, remembering to show his shield, sandals, helmet, etc.

Exercise 1.2

1. (a) Explain the events leading up to Jason setting off on the voyage to gain the Golden Fleece.
    (b) Why might the Ancient Greeks have enjoyed hearing about Jason's adventures?
2. (a) Explain how Jason won the Golden Fleece.
    (b) Do you approve or disapprove of Medea's actions? Why?
3. (a) What did Jason do to gain the title of a hero? (Consider the whole story, not just his winning of the Golden Fleece.)
    (b) Give two possible reasons for saying that Jason was *not* a great hero.

Extension work

Which hero do you think was the greatest – Perseus, Jason or Theseus? Why do you think this? Write a speech to deliver to your class defending your choice of hero. Consider the help they received (from gods and mortals), the reasons for their actions, and their treatment of their fellow men and women.

Exercise 1.3

1. (a) Tell the story of Theseus's adventures on his way to Athens and when he met his father.
    (b) Name one good point about Theseus and one bad point about him.
2. (a) Tell the story of Theseus's most famous adventure. Make sure you include what happened to his father, Aegeus.
    (b) Do you think Ariadne deserved what happened to her? Give reasons for your answer.
3. (a) Which do you think was the hardest of all of Theseus's adventures? Give reasons for your answer.
    (b) What was Theseus's most impressive quality? Why do you think that it was important?

Extension work

Research in detail the various adventures of Theseus before and after he killed the Minotaur. Then, imagining that you are Theseus, write your autobiography, remembering to explain what your reasons were for your various actions.

CHAPTER 2 THE LABOURS OF HERACLES

2.1 The Labours of Heracles: 1–4

Heracles was one of the most popular Greek heroes and he faced all kinds of dangers, from the moment of his birth. Heracles's father was Zeus and his mother was a mortal princess, called Alcmene. The name *Hera-cles* means 'glory of Hera', but actually Zeus's wife, Hera, was furious that her husband had fathered Heracles by another woman. In her rage she sent two giant snakes to kill the boy. Heracles's twin brother, Iphicles, screamed in terror when he saw the serpents, but Heracles was completely fearless. Chuckling happily to himself, he took the snakes in his hands and strangled them.

Years later, Hera had her revenge when she drove Heracles insane. During his madness, Heracles killed his wife Megara, and their children. The gods decided that Heracles had to be punished and they ordered him to do whatever tasks his cousin King Eurystheus of Argos and Mycenae set him.

The First Labour – the Nemean lion

This Greek vase painting shows Heracles tackling the Nemean lion

Heracles's first task was to kill a terrible lion, which was ravaging the country around the city of Nemea. Lions are fearsome beasts at the best of times, but the Nemean lion was particularly hard to kill because no man-made weapon could penetrate its tough hide. Heracles threw spears, but they bounced off; he shot arrows, but they did not harm the lion; Heracles even attempted to stun it with his club, but the creature ignored the blows. Eventually, Heracles followed the lion into its den and tried to strangle it with his bare hands. The beast roared and rampaged round the cave, but Heracles clung on until he overpowered it.

Looking at the dead beast, Heracles thought that its skin would make a fine cloak. After blunting several weapons trying to pierce the skin, he used the lion's own claws to cut through the tough hide. Wrapping himself in his new cloak, Heracles returned triumphantly to the city. However, when Eurystheus learned of Heracles's success, he was so frightened of his cousin that he forbade Heracles to enter the city again.

The Second Labour – the Hydra of Lerna

The Lernaean Hydra was so dangerous that even the touch of its breath could kill a man. The monster had the body of a dog out of which grew many snake heads. The Hydra lived in a swamp near Lerna, in Argos, and it was protected by a giant crab which attacked anyone who approached. Heracles easily crushed the crab, but the Hydra was much harder to tackle. Heracles tried to kill it with his club, but whenever he killed one head, two or three grew in its place.

Heracles realised that he had to prevent the heads from re-growing, otherwise he would never overcome the monster. Fortunately, Heracles was accompanied by his nephew, Iolaus. Heracles ordered Iolaus to burn the stump of each head after he had cut it off. The heat of the fire seared the wounds and stopped the heads from growing back. Eventually, only the main head was left and Heracles hacked through its neck with a great blow from his sword. The Lernaean Hydra lay dead, and Heracles dipped his arrows in its blood, coating them in potent poison. Now, even a mere scratch would inflict certain death.

The Third Labour – the Ceryneian hind

Heracles's Third Labour was to capture the Ceryneian hind alive. This beautiful deer had golden horns and bronze hooves. It was sacred to Artemis and could run so swiftly that an entire year passed before Heracles caught up with it. Heracles then had to capture it without harming it. Taking an un-poisoned arrow from his quiver, he shot skilfully through the front legs of the deer. With its forelegs pinned together, the hind could no longer flee; Heracles easily caught it and tied its legs together. Artemis appeared and angrily demanded to know why he was taking the hind. Heracles explained that Eurystheus had ordered him to do it, so he was allowed to return unscathed to Mycenae.

The Fourth Labour – the Erymanthian boar

The Erymanthian boar was an enormous, vicious creature which lived in Arcadia. It had huge tusks and could easily rip a man apart. Nonetheless, Heracles was ordered to capture it alive. Heracles first tracked the boar down to its hiding place in a vast thicket of thorny bushes. Eventually, he drove it out of the thicket and chased it into a snowdrift, where it could not move so quickly. Heracles jumped onto the boar's back and, before it could slice his arms with its tusks, he bound it in strong chains. Then he dragged it alive back to Mycenae.

2.2 The Labours of Heracles: 5–8

The Fifth Labour – the Augean stables

Heracles's most disgusting adventure was when he had to clean the stables of Augeas, the King of Elis. Augeas owned a vast number of sheep and cattle, but he never had their stables cleaned. The filth and dung created by so many animals had piled up over the years and the smell was so revolting that crops no longer grew in the nearby valleys because the air had been contaminated.

Augeas agreed that he would give Heracles some of his animals if Heracles cleaned the stables in a single day. The stables were far too filthy for one man to clean alone, so Heracles used Nature to help him. He diverted the nearby rivers Alpheus and Peneus so that they ran through the stables and washed out the years of accumulated grime. However, when Heracles came to claim his reward, Augeas refused to pay. '*You* didn't clean the stables, the rivers did,' he claimed. 'So I shan't pay you!' And to make things worse, Eurystheus also claimed that the rivers had done the work, not Heracles, and so refused to count the Labour. In revenge, Heracles invaded Elis, killed Augeas and placed his son Phyleus, who had supported Heracles's claim to a reward, on the throne.

The Sixth Labour – the Stymphalian birds

The Sixth Labour saw Heracles tackle the vicious man-eating birds of the Stymphalian marsh. Hundreds of these birds lived near the marsh, all with bronze claws, beaks and wings. Heracles's task was to drive them away from the region but it was very difficult to approach the birds because the marsh was too watery to walk on, yet too solid for a boat to sail through. Heracles, therefore, decided to scare the birds into the air, where it would be easier to attack them. Athene had given Heracles a pair of bronze castanets and he shook these vigorously. The loud noise frightened the birds and, as they flew up into the sky, Heracles killed many of them with his arrows. Fortunately, the rest of them were too frightened to return to land and flew off to the Isle of Ares in the Black Sea.

The Seventh Labour – the Cretan bull

Heracles's Seventh Labour was to capture the Cretan bull. This huge bull breathed fire and was rampaging across Crete, destroying crops and killing people. Although King Minos of Crete offered to help Heracles, Heracles had to refuse his aid because

Eurystheus had ordered him to catch the bull single-handed.

Heracles pursued the fire-breathing bull for a long time before he was able to overpower it and drag it back to Mycenae. Eurystheus dedicated the bull to Hera, but the goddess still hated Heracles and was incensed at being given a gift which demonstrated how skilful and brave Heracles was. Hera furiously drove the bull all the way from Mycenae to Athens, where the hero Theseus sacrificed it to Athene.

The Eighth Labour – the horses of Diomedes

Heracles had faced many man-eating monsters and deadly wild animals. However, in his Eighth Labour, he faced the unusual threat of four savage mares that had been trained to eat human flesh. These horses belonged to Diomedes, the king of Thrace in Northern Greece, and were so violent that they were normally kept tied up to bronze mangers by iron chains. Many Greek kings liked to show off their horses to their guests, but Diomedes's idea of hospitality was to feed his guests alive to his mares. Diomedes fully intended Heracles to die in this way, but Heracles overpowered Diomedes's grooms. Then he let loose the mares and drove them down to the sea.

At this point, Diomedes gathered his servants together and counter-attacked. It looked as if Heracles would be outnumbered, but he cut a channel from the shore so that the sea flooded through it onto the plain. Seeing the advancing torrents, Diomedes's servants fled, abandoning their ruthless king. Heracles stunned Diomedes with his club and then fed him to his own horses. After the mares had satisfied their hunger by eating their master, they became controllable. Heracles then led the mares to Mycenae, where Eurystheus dedicated them to Hera, and set them free.

2.3 The Labours of Heracles: 9–12

The Ninth Labour – the girdle of Hippolyta

Heracles's next adventure saw him pitted against the Amazons. These were a race of warrior women who ruled the land and fought wars while their menfolk did the household tasks. The queen of the Amazons was Hippolyta. Ares, the god of war, admired Hippolyta so much that he gave her a golden girdle which she wore round her waist. King Eurystheus ordered Heracles to fetch this girdle.

Heracles knew of the Amazons' reputation as great warriors, so he approached them with care. At first, things went well. Hippolyta admired Heracles greatly and happily offered him her girdle as a gift. However, jealous Hera was furious that Heracles was succeeding so easily. She decided to make the quest much harder and deliberately spread a rumour that Heracles was planning to abduct Hippolyta. The outraged Amazons charged angrily towards Heracles's ship, screaming threats and waving weapons. Heracles thought that Hippolyta had entrapped him and, trying to escape, he killed her and many of the other Amazons. Heracles snatched Hippolyta's girdle from her corpse and took it back to Eurystheus, who gave it to his daughter, Admete.

The Tenth Labour – the cattle of Geryon

Heracles's Tenth Labour was to steal the cattle that belonged to Geryon, the strongest man on earth. Geryon was not merely powerful; he also had three heads, six hands and three bodies joined together at the waist. If defeating Geryon were not enough of a challenge, his cattle were also guarded by Eurytion, the son of Ares, and a two-headed watchdog called Orthrus.

The cattle of Geryon were grazing peacefully when Heracles approached them. The watchdog, Orthrus, smelt Heracles and, barking loudly, raced towards him. Heracles slew Orthrus with his club and then promptly killed Eurytion, who had been alerted by Orthrus's snarling. Both guards lay dead on the ground, so Heracles started to drive off the cattle. Suddenly, with a bloodcurdling roar, the fearsome Geryon appeared. Heracles knew that he would be crushed to death if Geryon managed to catch him, so he grabbed his bow and quickly loosed off an arrow. Heracles's aim was so accurate that the arrow passed through all three of Geryon's bodies. Meanwhile Hera, who was watching the fight, tried to help Geryon, but Heracles wounded her with another arrow. Having defeated two guards, a three-headed man and a goddess, Heracles was now free to lead the cattle off to Eurystheus.

The Eleventh Labour – the apples of the Hesperides

The gods had commanded Heracles to carry out ten Labours. Therefore, after completing his Tenth Labour, Heracles asked Eurystheus to let him go. However, King Eurystheus mocked his request: 'You had help from Iolaus when you killed the Hydra and the stables of Augeas were cleaned by the rivers, not you. Those Labours don't count – I shall set you two more! Your next task is to fetch the fruit from the golden apple tree which Earth gave as a wedding present to Hera.'

Heracles knew that this apple tree was somewhere in Hera's garden on Mount Atlas and that it was tended by the Hesperides, the daughters of Hesperus (the Evening Star). However, for a long time Heracles searched for the tree in vain. Finally, he seized Nereus, the river god, and forced Nereus to tell how to find the apples. Nereus warned Heracles that the apples were guarded by a fierce dragon, called Ladon, which lay coiled around the tree. 'You must kill Ladon,' he advised Heracles, 'but you will not be able to pluck the apples from the tree yourself. Instead, send the giant Atlas to fetch them.'

Heracles killed Ladon without much difficulty and Atlas happily agreed to help Heracles. The only problem was that Atlas held up the sky on his shoulders and, if he let go, the world would be destroyed. Heracles volunteered to take on Atlas's job for an hour while Atlas went to fetch the apples. However, Atlas planned to leave Heracles to hold up the sky forever and, when he returned with the apples, he refused to take up his burden again. Heracles begged Atlas to hold the sky for one moment while he placed a cushion on his back. Foolishly, Atlas agreed. Heracles snatched the apples and left for Mycenae, leaving Atlas once more holding up the sky.

This Greek vase shows King Eurystheus hiding in terror from Cerberus

The Twelfth Labour – the capture of Cerberus

Heracles's final Labour was perhaps his hardest: he was ordered to descend to the Underworld and bring back Cerberus, the three-headed hound of Hell. Normally only the dead crossed the River Styx to Tartarus and Heracles must have known that he might easily become trapped in the Underworld, never to return to the land of the living.

Heracles travelled boldly over the River Styx and asked Hades, the ruler of the Underworld, to give him his guard dog, Cerberus. Hades agreed, but only if Heracles overcame Cerberus with his bare hands. This was a daunting prospect, for Cerberus's three heads all had manes of serpents and his tail was equipped with sharp barbs. Heracles carefully wrapped himself up in his impenetrable lion skin and choked Cerberus until the dog was forced to give in. Heracles dragged Cerberus away from the world of the dead and crossed back over the River Styx. When Heracles arrived at Mycenae, Eurystheus was so frightened of the sight of Cerberus that he jumped into a large oil jar and ordered Heracles to return the dog to Hades.

Exercise 2.1

1. (a) Describe Heracles's early life and explain why he had to undertake the Labours.
    (b) Was it fair that Heracles had to undertake his Labours?
2. (a) Describe either the First or Second Labour of Heracles and explain how he completed his task.
    (b) Did Heracles show any other qualities apart from bravery? Explain your answer.
3. (a) Tell the story of the Ceryneian hind and the Erymanthian boar.
    (b) Which task would you prefer to be ordered to do and why do you think this?

Extension work

The Labours of Heracles were a very popular subject for Greek vase painters. Research examples of these vases and EITHER give a presentation on them to your class (including information on different pottery styles and shapes as well as the different myths) OR design your own vase modelled on Greek styles.

Exercise 2.2

1. (a) Tell the story of the Augean stables.
    (b) Do you think Augeas's reaction to Heracles's success was reasonable? Explain your answer.
2. (a) What happened when Heracles tackled the Stymphalian birds and the Cretan bull?
    (b) If you had been Hera, how would you have reacted to the dedication of the Cretan bull and why would you have reacted like this?
3. (a) Describe the events of Heracles's Eighth Labour (the horses of Diomedes).
    (b) Do you think Heracles treated Diomedes fairly? Explain your answer.

Extension work

Play 'Heracles Snap'.

Design twelve cards to illustrate the Labours of Heracles.

Make four copies of each Labour.

Then play 'Snap' as per normal rules with two options, using either option or both:

(a)   when you call out 'Snap' you must follow it with the name of the Labour illustrated

(b)   when you call out 'Snap' you must give a quick summary of the Labour.

Exercise 2.3

1. (a)   Narrate what happened when Heracles met Hippolyta.
    (b)   Heracles was one of the most popular heroes in Greek mythology. Why do you think that Greeks might have preferred to hear about his adventures, rather than those of another hero?

2. (a)   Tell the stories of how Heracles tackled Geryon and Cerberus.
    (b)   Which do you think was the more fearsome opponent and why do you think this?

3. (a)   Describe in detail the events of Heracles' Eleventh Labour (the apples of the Hesperides).
    (b)   Was it fair that Heracles had to carry out two extra Labours? Why do you think this?

Extension work

Carry out further investigation into Heracles's entire career (not just the Labours). Decide whether he was a great hero or a brainless thug and then write an essay arguing your case.

CHAPTER 3 THE TROJAN WAR

3.1 The judgement of Paris

Helen was the most beautiful mortal in the whole world, but her beauty did not bring much happiness. The Trojan War was fought for her sake and she was to go down in history as 'the face that launched a thousand ships'.

The first trigger for the war was Eris, the goddess of strife. Eris was a very jealous goddess and she was unpopular with the other gods because she deliberately caused discontent wherever she went. Thus it was not surprising that Eris did not receive an invitation to the marriage of the nymph Thetis to the mortal Peleus. However, Eris was furious at this insult and plotted her revenge. She threw a beautiful golden apple into the hall where all the immortals were feasting. On the apple were inscribed the words 'For the Fairest'. Naturally, all the goddesses thought that the apple must be meant for them! After a long argument, three powerful goddesses were left claiming the apple: Athene, the goddess of wisdom; Aphrodite, the goddess of love; and Hera, wife of Zeus, the king of the gods. They demanded that Zeus decide which of them deserved the apple, but he refused. He knew that the two goddesses who were not chosen would be furious with him and he wanted to avoid trouble. Instead, he summoned the messenger god, Hermes, and told him to ask a trustworthy mortal to make the judgement.

Hermes's choice fell on Paris, son of Priam and Hecuba, the king and queen of Troy. Hermes ordered Paris to decide which of the three goddesses was the most beautiful; then he flew off, leaving Paris to make his judgement. The goddesses appeared, but they were reluctant to trust to their beauty alone. First Hera came to Paris and offered him great wealth and power if he would say that she was the most fair. Then Athene said that she would give him great wisdom. Finally,

This 2nd century AD mosaic from Turkey shows the three goddesses assembled before Paris

Aphrodite promised to give Paris the most beautiful woman in the world if he chose her. All of these bribes had their attractions, but Paris wanted a very beautiful wife, so he gave the golden apple to Aphrodite.

Aphrodite revealed that the most beautiful woman in the world was Helen, the wife of King Menelaus of Sparta. Paris travelled to Sparta with Aphrodite's help and was welcomed warmly by Menelaus. However, while Menelaus was away, Paris seduced Helen and set sail with her – and much of Menelaus's gold – back to Troy. Menelaus was extremely angry and turned to his brother Agamemnon, the king of Mycenae, for help. Now, before Helen and Menelaus got married, so many Greek princes had wanted to marry Helen that Helen's father had feared that one of them might abduct her. Therefore each of her suitors had sworn an oath that they would return Helen to her rightful husband if anyone ever stole her. Agamemnon now summoned all of Helen's former suitors and told them to gather their followers and prepare for war. Soon, a huge Greek army set off to Troy to recover Helen. This was the beginning of the Trojan War.

3.2 The wrath of Achilles and the death of Patroclus

The Greeks were united in their desire to bring Helen (and, ideally, lots of loot) back from Troy. However, they often disagreed as to how to conduct the war. This lack of unity became very clear when, in the tenth year of the war, Achilles, the best Greek warrior, quarrelled with Agamemnon, the leader of the Greeks.

In Greek warfare, it was normal practice for captured women and children to be enslaved. One of the many slaves captured by Greek raiding parties was a girl called Chryseis, whose father, Chryses, was a priest of Apollo. Chryses came to the Greek camp and begged Agamemnon, who held his daughter captive, to let the girl return home. Agamemnon refused angrily and told Chryses to leave the camp immediately. Chryses realised that Agamemnon would not relent and he prayed to Apollo to take revenge on the Greeks. Apollo heard his priest's words and sent a deadly plague into the Greek camp. Men and horses sickened and died. Finally the Greek soothsayer Calchas warned Agamemnon that he must return Chryseis to her father. Reluctantly Agamemnon agreed, but he decided to take Achilles's slave girl, Briseis, as a replacement for the girl whom he had lost.

Achilles was so angry that he refused to fight for the Greeks any more. The news of his defection spread rapidly. The Greeks' morale plummeted when they learned of the loss of their best fighter and the Trojans rejoiced as they inflicted several defeats on Agamemnon's forces. In desperation, Agamemnon sent envoys to plead for Achilles to return to battle and Achilles's best friend, Patroclus, also begged him to help the Greeks. But Achilles still resented Agamemnon's high-handed actions and refused to fight.

Patroclus realised that, without Achilles fighting for them, the Greeks might soon lose the war and he devised a cunning plan to boost Greek morale. Patroclus was a good fighter and he decided to wear Achilles's armour into battle. If the Greeks thought that Achilles had returned to the fray then they would fight much better, but the Trojans would be greatly demoralised. Achilles agreed to Patroclus's plan, but warned him not to advance too far forward on his own. Patroclus was initially successful and a determined charge drove back the Trojans. However, he forgot Achilles's advice and was soon confronted by Hector, son of King Priam of Troy. Hector cut Patroclus down and stripped off his armour, revealing the deception.

When the news of Patroclus's death reached the Greek camp, Achilles went mad with grief and guilt. Waiting only until he had acquired new armour from Hephaestos, the blacksmith god, he marched out the next day, intent upon revenge. Cleaving his way through the Trojans, he came up against Hector. Hector tried to flee but could not escape swift-footed Achilles. As he lay dying, Hector pleaded for Achilles to give his body to his parents for burial. Achilles contemptuously retorted: 'The dogs and vultures will maul your body; indeed, I wish that I could eat you raw for what you have done to me.' Achilles then tied Hector's body to his chariot and every day he drove three times round the walls of Troy with Hector's noble head dragging in the dust behind him. Soon the gods grew angry with Achilles and sent his mother, Thetis, to order him to give the body back. Achilles listened to her and when Priam himself came to beg Achilles to return his son's corpse, Achilles remembered his own father, Peleus, and took pity on the old man. Raising Priam from his knees, Achilles wept with him before giving up Hector's body to the Trojan king.

3.3 The wooden horse

Although the Greeks were valiant fighters, so were the Trojans. Moreover, they had a good defensive position because the city of Troy was surrounded by strong, high walls. After ten long years of war, the Greeks were despairing of ever defeating the Trojans. At this point a particularly cunning Greek, called Odysseus, came up with an ingenious plan. He pointed out that the Greeks had tried to capture Troy by force of arms, but had failed. Now was the time to try trickery.

Odysseus suggested that the Greeks should build an enormous horse out of wood and fill it with their bravest warriors. The other Greeks would leave the horse outside the walls of Troy, as if it were an offering to the gods, and then pretend to sail away. The Greeks agreed to try this trick and rapidly built the wooden horse.

One morning the Trojans woke up to discover that there was no sign of the Greek army. The camp was deserted, the ships had gone from the harbour and all that could be seen was an enormous wooden horse near the gates of the city. Unable to believe that the war was finally over, the Trojans sent out reconnaissance parties to check whether the Greeks were in hiding. Before long they found a Greek soldier called Sinon. Sinon claimed that he had deserted from the Greek army because Odysseus had been planning to murder him. When questioned about the wooden horse, Sinon replied that it was a gift to the gods from the Greeks.

At this point, some of the Trojans suggested that they should destroy the horse, while others wanted to bring it into the city and dedicate it to the gods as a gift from the Trojans. Sinon said that a Greek soothsayer had predicted that, if the Trojans brought the horse into the city, they would be able to sail to Greece and capture Mycenae. Hearing this, the Trojans were delighted and started to drag the heavy offering into the city. However, one Trojan called Laocoon tried to stop them. 'I fear the Greeks, even when they come bearing gifts,' he shouted. Some of the Trojans paused, but suddenly a giant sea serpent appeared, swimming vigorously towards the shore. As the horrified onlookers watched, the sea monster came onto the land, wrapped its coils round Laocoon and his two sons and crushed them to death. The shocked Trojans thought that the gods were angry with Laocoon for wanting to destroy the horse. Now, certain that the horse was a good omen, the doomed Trojans brought it into the city amidst great rejoicing.

This 2nd or 1st century BC sculpture of the serpent crushing Laocoon and his sons can be found in the Vatican City

The Trojans held a great feast to celebrate the end of the ten-year war. The feast lasted well into the night, until everyone was either drunk or asleep. The Greek plan then came into effect. The armed soldiers who had hidden all day inside the wooden horse crept out silently, dropping one by one onto the ground. They opened the city gates and let in the other Greeks, who had sailed back under cover of darkness. When all the troops were gathered, the slaughter began. Greeks charged through the streets, mercilessly cutting down everyone they found, with no respect for age or gender. They even killed King Priam at the altar where he had fled for protection. By daybreak, Troy was in ruins. Those who were still alive were enslaved and dragged to the ships to begin their journey into captivity in Greece. Only a few Trojans managed to escape, led by Prince Aeneas.

With Troy destroyed, the surviving Greeks set off home. Not all were as fortunate as Menelaus, who found Helen, forgave her and returned with her to Sparta. His brother Agamemnon reached Mycenae, only to be murdered by his wife, Clytemnestra. Many other Greeks perished in shipwrecks and it took Odysseus, whose ingenuity had led to the fall of Troy, ten years to reach his island home of Ithaca.

Exercise 3.1

1. (a) Describe why the judgement of Paris occurred and what the judgement was.
   (b) Which goddess would you have chosen if you had been Paris? Explain why you would have made that decision.
2. (a) Explain what happened after Paris made his judgement and how the Trojan War started.
   (b) Do you think that Menelaus was correct to go to war over a woman? Why?

Extension work

Write EITHER the prosecution OR the defence speech in a lawsuit brought against Paris for starting the Trojan War. You will need to consider who else might have been held responsible.

Exercise 3.2

1. (a) Explain in detail why Achilles refused to fight for the Greek forces any more.
   (b) If you had been Achilles would you have refused to fight for Agamemnon? Why?
2. (a) Tell the story of the death of Patroclus.
   (b) Name one good quality that Achilles showed and one bad quality.

Extension work

Write a poem exploring Priam's feelings as he approaches the Greek camp to beg for Hector's body to be released.

Exercise 3.3

1. (a) Explain how the Greeks eventually managed to capture Troy.
   (b) What lesson do you think the Greeks drew from the fall of Troy? Why?

2. (a) Imagine you are a Trojan. Tell the story of what happened on the final night of the Trojan War.

(b) Why do you think that the Trojans may have believed that the wooden horse was a gift, not a trap? Give reasons.

Extension work

The story of the Trojan horse was very popular in Roman times and the phrase *timeo Danaos et dona ferentes* ('I fear Greeks, even when they come bearing gifts') is still used today. EITHER design a poster to illustrate this phrase OR make your own 3-D model of the wooden horse.

CHAPTER 4 THE WANDERINGS OF ODYSSEUS

After the fall of Troy, Odysseus and his men faced many amazing adventures on their way home to the island of Ithaca. Greek ships were small and relied on their sails or oars to negotiate the seas. Storms could blow up without warning and sea captains preferred to stay within easy reach of land. Ships could not carry many supplies so it was often necessary to land and search for fresh water. Several of Odysseus's adventures took place during such expeditions.

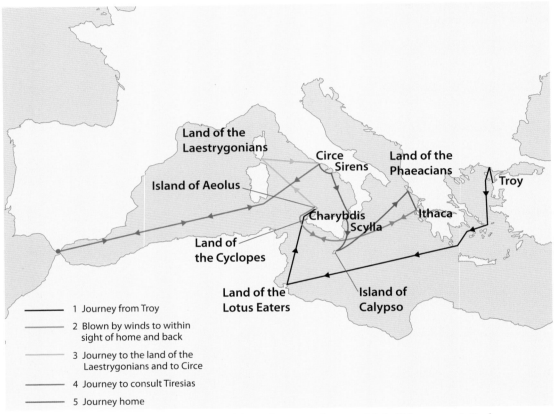

The voyages of Odysseus: although some places which Odysseus visited are real (e.g. Troy), many other places are uncertain

4.1 The land of the lotus eaters

One of Odysseus's first adventures occurred shortly after his ships left Troy. The flotilla landed at an unknown island and Odysseus sent three men inland in search of food and water. After some time the men had not returned and Odysseus began to suspect the worst. He gathered a search party and set off after them. To his surprise he soon found his men, not the prisoners of a hostile tribe as he had feared, but eating and drinking with the locals and clearly very content. Nevertheless, Odysseus was deeply concerned when the inhabitants told him that he had reached the land of the lotus eaters. He knew that whoever ate the lotus flower forgot all his cares and lost any desire to return home.

The friendly inhabitants offered refreshments to Odysseus and his companions. Odysseus refused and forbade his companions from eating anything. Instead, he ordered them to seize the three who had eaten the lotus. Protesting loudly, the three sailors were dragged back to the ships. Odysseus weighed anchor and set sail at once. As the ships left the island, the effect of the lotus wore off and the drugged sailors slowly regained their memory.

4.2 The Cyclops Polyphemus

Odysseus next came to the land of the Cyclopes. These fearsome giants had only a single eye in the middle of their forehead and towered over ordinary men. The land of the Cyclopes was not the best place to go searching for provisions, but Odysseus did not know where he had landed when he set off to find food and water. Odysseus and twelve of his men were marching through the countryside when they discovered a large cave in a hill. Entering it, they found that it was well stocked with all kinds of delicious food – huge cheeses, supplies of milk and other delicacies. The men wanted to take some supplies and leave immediately, but Odysseus was consumed by curiosity and wished to find out who had gathered such abundant stocks of food. Odysseus commanded his men to wait until they had met the farmer who owned the cave, but this decision was a dreadful mistake. When the owner returned, he led his flock of giant sheep into the cave, then slammed a huge rock over the entrance. The Greeks looked up in horror as they realised that the owner of the cave was not a friendly farmer, but the Cyclops Polyphemus!

This 6th century BC vase painting shows Odysseus and his men ramming the olive-wood stake into Polyphemus's single eye

Polyphemus soon caught sight of the Greeks and asked them what they were doing in his cave. Odysseus explained that they were sailors returning to Greece after the end of the Trojan War. He boldly added: 'I claim hospitality in the name of Zeus, the protector of travellers.' The Cyclops's booming laugh echoed round the cave. 'I care naught for the gods, they are nothing to us!' Then he seized two of Odysseus's men, dashed out their brains on the rocky floor and ate them.

When the Cyclops fell asleep, the terrified Greeks discussed their plight. They could have killed Polyphemus that night, but Odysseus realised that they needed Polyphemus alive to move the boulder that blocked the entrance to the cave. This rock was so heavy that mere men could not move it. When morning came, the Cyclops breakfasted on two more of Odysseus's crew. Then he led his sheep out to pasture, carefully blocking up the cave's entrance behind him. Odysseus now told his remaining men what he intended to do. First, they sharpened a long stake made from olive wood and hardened the point off in the fire. Then they hid it out of Polyphemus's sight.

At dusk the Greeks heard the tramping of the giant's feet as he returned with his flock. They tried to hide, but the Cyclops soon found them and ate two more men for dinner. Now Odysseus put the second part of his plan into action. Standing up boldly in the middle of the cave, he offered Polyphemus some wine. Polyphemus took the wine and drank a long draught. The Cyclops enjoyed the taste and thanked Odysseus, asking him what his name was. Odysseus answered that he was called 'Nobody' and offered the Cyclops more wine. Polyphemus drank deeply; soon the wine overpowered him and he fell asleep. Odysseus and his remaining men took the stake from its hiding place and drove it into the Cyclops's single eye, twisting it round and round like a drill. Polyphemus woke up, blinded and in agony. Again and again he screamed out in pain and soon the other Cyclopes hurried to ask what was wrong. 'Aaaaah,' he shrieked. 'Nobody is hurting me. Nobody has blinded me.' The other Cyclopes could not understand what Polyphemus meant and, thinking that he was either mad or drunk, they left him alone.

The next morning, Polyphemus had to let out his sheep. He knew that the Greeks might try to escape, so he sat in the mouth of the cave and carefully felt the back of each sheep to ensure that no one was riding on them. However, Odysseus had thought of this and had yoked the sheep together in groups of three. Under the middle sheep in each group was tied a Greek and Odysseus himself clung underneath the enormous ram of the flock.

Thus the Greeks escaped from Polyphemus. They raced for their ship and set sail as quickly as possibly. Suddenly, the Cyclops appeared on top of a cliff, blindly hurling rocks in their direction and cursing 'Nobody'. Odysseus was proud and he wanted Polyphemus to know who had outwitted him. Standing up in the boat he yelled, 'Know this, Cyclops, it was not Nobody who blinded you, but Odysseus, son of Laertes, sacker of cities!' Greek heroes always boasted of their deeds, and Polyphemus now knew Odysseus's real name. He lost no time in praying to his father Poseidon, the sea god, to avenge him. From that moment on, Poseidon would be Odysseus's implacable enemy.

4.3 Aeolus and the winds

After escaping from the murderous Cyclops, Odysseus and his men fled until they reached the island of Aeolus, the ruler of the winds. Aeolus was friendly and the crews rested for some time, enjoying his hospitality. When the time of departure came, Aeolus gave Odysseus a large leather sack, commanding him not to open it until he was safely home. After they had been sailing for several days, the sailors noticed that Odysseus never let the bag out of his sight and never let anyone else touch it. The sailors grew very jealous, thinking that Aeolus must have given Odysseus a great treasure. 'Why should Odysseus have all of these riches?' they asked. 'Surely Aeolus meant us all to share it?'

Eventually, the Greek ships were nearing Ithaca when Odysseus, exhausted by the effort of constantly commanding the ship, lay down to sleep. The greedy sailors seized their chance and opened the bag, expecting to find jewels, gold coins and silver goblets. Instead, much to their surprise, there was a wild rushing sound and a

terrible storm blew up, driving the ships back to the Isle of Aeolus. The sack had contained all the winds but one, the west wind, which had gently blown Odysseus and his men home to Ithaca.

Odysseus and the sailors begged Aeolus to help them once more, but he curtly refused. 'I shall not help those who are clearly cursed by the gods,' he retorted. 'You are the enemies of the gods – find your own way home!'

4.4 The land of the man-eating Laestrygonians

Odysseus had managed to escape from the man-eating Cyclops Polyphemus with the loss of only a few companions. However, his adventure with the Laestrygonians led to a much higher death toll.

After leaving the Isle of Aeolus for the second time, Odysseus and his companions sailed for some time without a break. They were eager to rest and so, when they spotted what appeared to be a good place to anchor their ships, they drew them up in the shadow of some high cliffs. Next, the Greeks sent some reconnaissance parties to

29

the shore. However, the ships had been observed by the inhabitants of this region – the Laestrygonians. These creatures were not friendly farmers, but a race of savage cannibals. The Laestrygonians were delighted to see some new prey anchored below the cliffs where they lived. They swiftly seized huge rocks and hurled them down onto the ships. All but one of the ships were sunk and the Laestrygonians climbed down to the beach where they snatched the sailors as they swam to the shore and ate them. Only the crew of one ship, urged on by Odysseus, managed to escape the dreadful fate of being eaten alive.

4.5 Odysseus meets the goddess Circe and travels to the Underworld

After the encounter with the cannibal Laestrygonians, Odysseus had only one ship left and most of his men had been slaughtered. The remainder must have started to fear that they would never return home and their encounter with the enchantress Circe would not have improved their morale.

At first, all went well. Odysseus's ship landed at a beautiful island and the men disembarked happily. Odysseus's lieutenant, Eurylochus, volunteered to lead a band of sailors inland to explore, while Odysseus remained with the rest, guarding the ship. Eurylochus led the men through the lush vegetation until they saw smoke rising above the trees and heard a woman singing. Creeping closer, they saw a fine house in the middle of a clearing in the forest. The men were surprised to see a large number of wild animals wandering around near the house. Moreover, they were amazed when a beautiful woman appeared and greeted the animals in a most friendly manner, stroking the lions and patting the wolves.

The Greeks decided that they had arrived at the home of a goddess and went forward to introduce themselves. Circe was delighted to see the men. 'You are very welcome at my palace. You must be in need of refreshment and rest – come inside and dine with me before you return to your ship, laden with food.'

The men happily accepted, but Eurylochus was suspicious and remained outside. Looking through the windows he saw his companions enjoying a wonderful feast. He was considering joining them when he saw something peculiar happening. The men were growing large ears and their noses were turning into snouts; their hands had become trotters and all of them had curly tails. Circe had turned the men into pigs! As Eurylochus stared, appalled at what he had seen, the door suddenly opened and Circe appeared. She drove the pigs out of the palace and commanded them: 'Be off to the sty and wallow in the mud!' Then she returned indoors, leaving the pigs grunting and rolling about on the ground.

Eurylochus rushed back to the ship to report to Odysseus, who decided that he must try to rescue his men. As he hurried through the forest, a stranger appeared in front of him. Odysseus halted and the stranger spoke to him.

'Greetings, Odysseus, son of Laertes. The gods have sent me, Hermes, to warn you that Circe is a witch. You cannot withstand her spells unless you are armed with a certain magical flower, known as moly. Take this moly and approach Circe with caution!'

Odysseus thanked Hermes for his warning and took the moly gratefully. Then he continued to Circe's palace.

When Odysseus reached the palace, Circe smiled sweetly at him and offered him wine. Odysseus drank her magical potion in one go, but when Circe tried to cast a spell on him, she got a shock. Instead of turning into an animal, Odysseus seized his sword and threatened to kill Circe unless she undid the spell on his men. Circe realised that Odysseus

must be protected by the gods and she gave in. She turned Odysseus's companions back into their human form and all the other animals too, then held a year-long banquet to make up for what she had done to them.

Over the course of the next year, Odysseus spent a lot of time talking to Circe about his return home. Circe knew a considerable amount of magical lore and she advised Odysseus to visit the Underworld to ask the seer Tiresias for advice about his journey home. However, Odysseus first had to carry out certain rites to ensure he was able to reach the Underworld. He made the long journey to Persephone's grove and then walked inland to where three rivers met. Beside the banks of the River Acheron he dug a trench and sacrificed a ram and a black ewe to Hades and Persephone. The warm blood of the sheep ran into the trench and the smell attracted the ghosts of the dead, who knew that the blood could bring them back to life for a short time. However, Odysseus refused to let any of the ghosts drink the blood before he had spoken to Tiresias. The prophet warned Odysseus that Poseidon had not forgiven him for blinding Polyphemus.

'Poseidon still seeks revenge and will harm you if he can. You must sacrifice to him and try to avert his anger. Moreover, you face other dangers: you must on no account harm the cattle of the sun god and you must be vigilant when you return home to Ithaca, for your enemies lie in wait.'

With these warnings ringing in his ears, Odysseus returned to Circe.

4.6 The Sirens and Scylla and Charybdis

After the year spent with Circe, Odysseus set off for home. Circe had warned him that he would have to sail past the island of the Sirens. These creatures had the faces of beautiful girls, the bodies of birds, and wondrous voices, which bewitched all who heard them. Perched high up on the cliffs, they sang their enchanting songs and lured sailors to their doom on the rocks below.

Circe had advised Odysseus to block his and his sailors' ears with beeswax so they could not hear the Sirens singing. In this way, the crew would sail safely out of danger. However, Odysseus was determined to hear the Sirens' beautiful song and so he ordered his men to tie him to the mast before blocking their ears with wax. As the craft sailed past the cliffs where the Sirens lived, Odysseus could hear their sweet songs. Desperate to throw himself overboard so he could swim closer to the Sirens, Odysseus ranted and raved at his crew, demanding that they untie him. However, they could not hear him and ignored his pleas. They carried on sailing until they were

well out of earshot of the Sirens and then released their leader. Odysseus was the only mortal ever to hear the Sirens' song and survive. Some versions of the myth state that the Sirens were so angry at Odysseus's escape that they threw themselves off their cliffs onto the rocks, and died.

Shortly after sailing past the Sirens, Odysseus had to face the monsters Scylla and Charybdis. Charybdis was a giant whirlpool – ships which were caught by her were sucked down to the bottom of the sea and their crews eaten. Scylla was a dog-like monster with six heads and twelve feet who snatched sailors out of their ships and slowly swallowed them alive. It was

This 5th century BC Greek vase shows Odysseus tied to the mast whilst the Sirens fly down

difficult to escape both monsters as they were located very close to each other. Odysseus carefully steered round Charybdis, but sailed too close to Scylla. The crew watched aghast as Scylla's six heads swooped down on the boat, seized six of the men and began to devour them alive. Odysseus was unable to save these victims and his ship sailed on, the crew transfixed by the screams of terror still coming from their unfortunate comrades.

4.7 The cattle of the sun god and Calypso

When Odysseus visited the Underworld, the prophet Tiresias had delivered a very strong warning against harming the cattle of the sun god, no matter how desperate the Greeks might be. The cattle lived on the island of Thrinacia and, when Odysseus's ship approached the island, Odysseus wanted to sail straight past it. However, Odysseus's men were very tired and begged him to allow them to anchor the ship. They promised fervently that if Odysseus let them go ashore they would rest, but would not harm the cattle. Odysseus reluctantly gave way and the Greeks landed.

Now Fate intervened. When the Greeks reached Thrinacia the seas were calm and there was a gentle wind. However, once they had gone ashore, unfavourable winds blew up which prevented them from setting sail. Day after day, they were unable to leave and, after a month, their food had run out. The men grew desperate. Eventually, Eurylochus persuaded them that they had only one option if they were to avoid dying of starvation: they had to eat some of the cattle of the sun god. A few of the sailors remembered Odysseus's warnings and feared the consequences of killing the cattle, but Eurylochus promised that they would make amends immediately they reached Ithaca. Hungry and losing all hope of rescue, the men agreed and, while Odysseus was asleep, slaughtered some of the cattle. They then sat down to a stupendous feast. When Odysseus discovered what they had done, he was furious and refused to touch the sacred meat. The men laughed at his fears and continued to eat greedily.

Odysseus's men had been warned of the danger of their actions by their leader. Then the skeletons of the cattle began to walk about and low. At this point, any sensible person would have been terrified, but Odysseus's men ignored these frightening portents. They were soon to learn of their mistake.

The sun god, Helios (or Hyperion), was so angry at the killing of his cattle that he threatened never to shine upon the earth again unless the miscreants were punished. The other gods felt that his anger was justified and agreed to help. Suddenly, the winds dropped. The sailors rejoiced, thinking they could continue their journey. They cast off and sailed into deeper waters. Then Zeus struck, sending a dreadful tempest which destroyed Odysseus's ship. All of Odysseus's men perished in the waves.

Odysseus himself clung onto a piece of wood for ten days until he was blown onto the island of the nymph Calypso. She fell in love with him and refused to let him leave the island. Odysseus remained with Calypso for seven years until Zeus ordered her to let him leave. Odysseus built a huge raft and set sail. However, Poseidon still lusted for revenge and he destroyed the raft in a storm. Odysseus was lucky to escape by swimming to Drepane, the land of the Phaeacians. The next morning he was found by princess Nausicaa, who took him to her father, King Alcinous. Alcinous was delighted to meet the famous Odysseus and looked after him well. Eventually, he sent Odysseus home safely to Ithaca, loaded with gold and silver.

4.8 Odysseus's homecoming

When Odysseus finally reached Ithaca he did not set off immediately for his palace. Tiresias had warned him that his enemies would not be pleased if he returned and he wanted to discover what dangers awaited him. With Athene's help, Odysseus disguised himself as a beggar so that he could move round the countryside without being recognised. He soon found that he had a reliable ally in his swineherd, Eumaeus. Despite Odysseus's long absence, Eumaeus was still loyal and had tried to help Odysseus's son, Telemachus. Without telling Eumaeus who he was, Odysseus persuaded him to fetch Telemachus. Telemachus was delighted when Odysseus revealed his identity, but he warned his father that he had many enemies in Ithaca. In particular, Odysseus's wife, Penelope, was in danger of being married off to one of several men whom she hated.

Most people assumed that Odysseus had died many years ago and that Penelope was now a rich widow. Penelope was still beautiful, but the charms of her face were less important than the attraction of her wealth. Many men sought to marry Penelope and become rich by gaining control of Odysseus's land. However, Penelope did not want to remarry; she loved Odysseus and had no wish to choose one of the many suitors who congregated in Odysseus's palace, urging her to pick a new husband.

For many years, Penelope had been able to delay matters by claiming she had to weave a magnificent tapestry, which would be used as a burial shroud after her father-in-law, Laertes, died. Every night cunning Penelope unpicked what she had woven during the day and little progress was made on the tapestry. Eventually, a treacherous maid betrayed her plot to the suitors. Angry that a mere woman had tricked them for so long, the suitors insisted that Penelope swiftly finish the tapestry and then choose one of them as her new husband. Penelope was forced to agree, but she set a test for the suitors.

'I will marry the man who is equal to Odysseus. Let the one among you who is the best prove himself by doing what Odysseus once did – string his giant war-bow and shoot an arrow through twelve axe-rings.'

At this point, Odysseus made his way to the palace, still disguised as a poverty-stricken beggar. Penelope did not recognise her husband, but she was a kind woman and she ordered Odysseus's old nurse, Eurycleia, to wash the feet of the stranger. While Eurycleia bathed Odysseus, she recognised a scar on his thigh, which he had gained while hunting wild boar. Odysseus swore Eurycleia to silence, then entered the great hall to watch the contest of the bow. None of the suitors was able even to

string the bow and they were growing impatient and cross. Odysseus stepped forward, requesting to try his hand. The suitors sneered at the idea of a beggar succeeding when they had failed, but Odysseus strung the bow and shot the arrow through the twelve axe-rings. A shocked silence fell in the hall as the watchers realised that noble Odysseus had returned home. Then Odysseus exacted his revenge, shooting arrow after arrow at the suitors until they all lay dead on the floor. Only Phemius the bard and Medon the herald were spared.

After striking down the suitors, Odysseus had to persuade Penelope that he really was her husband. Penelope feared that he was an impostor, so set a test for him. She asked him to move Odysseus's

Only Odysseus was strong enough to draw the bow, as shown in this 5th century Greek vase painting

marriage bed out of their bedroom. Odysseus was angry with his wife. 'How can you ask me to do what is impossible?' he demanded, 'That bed was carved out of a living tree and cannot be moved!' Only Odysseus could have known this fact and Penelope realised with joy that her beloved husband had finally returned to her after an absence of twenty years.

Exercise 4

1. (a) Tell the story of what happened when Odysseus visited the land of the lotus eaters.
   (b) What do you think the men who had eaten the lotus flower might have thought when the drug wore off and why might they have thought this?
2. (a) Tell the story of Odysseus's encounter with the Cyclops.
   (b) Do you think that Polyphemus deserved his fate? Why?
3. (a) Narrate the story of Odysseus's encounter with Aeolus.
   (b) What moral do you think the Greeks might have drawn from this story?
4. (a) Tell the story of Odysseus's encounter with Circe.
   (b) How would you have dealt with Circe if you had been Odysseus and why?

5. (a) Outline what happened when Odysseus met the Laestrygonians; and then when he travelled to the Underworld.
   (b) Which adventure would you have found more frightening and why?
6. (a) Explain how Odysseus managed to avoid the Sirens and how he dealt with Scylla and Charybdis.
   (b) Name one good quality about Odysseus and one bad quality – explain the reasons for your answer.
7. (a) Narrate the story of Odysseus's adventures with the cattle of the sun god.
   (b) Do you think Odysseus's men deserved their fate? Why?
8. (a) State what happened when Odysseus met Calypso and what happened in one other of Odysseus's adventures.
   (b) Explain which adventure you think was the more difficult and why.
9. (a) Tell the story of Odysseus's homecoming.
   (b) Give two reasons why Greek women might have admired Penelope.

Extension work

1. Hold a class debate on whether Odysseus was a good leader. Write and present a speech for your side of the argument, making sure that you make detailed reference to Odysseus's adventures.

2. In many Greek myths the hero faces tests and challenges which he overcomes. Write an essay exploring what you think these stories suggest about what the Greeks valued in a hero. What sort of tests and challenges might we think makes someone heroic today?

3. The story of Odysseus's adventures was first told in Homer's *Odyssey*. Design an exciting illustration for the cover of a children's edition of *The Odyssey*. You may choose to illustrate the most exciting adventure or to create a collage of different adventures.

ROMANS

CHAPTER 5 EARLY ROMAN LEGENDS

5.1 Romulus and Remus and the founding of Rome (753 BC)

When Troy fell to the Greeks, most of the Trojan heroes were either killed or enslaved. One Trojan prince, however, escaped, and left the burning city with a small band of companions to begin a long voyage in search of a new Troy. This prince was Aeneas, and he eventually settled in Italy where he founded a city called Lavinium. His son, Iulus, wanted to build a city of his own, and so founded a city nearby, called Alba Longa. And it was here that the legendary founders of Rome were born.

Romulus and his twin brother Remus were the sons of Mars and Rhea Silvia. Mars was the god of war, but Rhea Silvia was a mortal woman, the daughter of King Numitor of Alba Longa. Numitor's younger brother, Amulius, was very ambitious and he seized the throne of Alba Longa. Once Amulius was king, he drove Numitor into exile and killed Numitor's sons. He was then faced with the problem of Numitor's daughter. Amulius did not want to risk unpopularity by putting a girl to death, but he was determined that she must not have any children who might grow up to avenge their grandfather. His solution was to force Rhea Silvia to become a Vestal Virgin. Vestals were very important priestesses who were not allowed to marry. However, even Amulius could not prevent Mars from falling in love with Rhea Silvia, and that is exactly what happened.

When Amulius learned that, despite all his precautions, Rhea Silvia had given birth to twin boys, he was incandescent with rage. He knew that when the twins were older they might want to help their grandfather, Numitor, or they might try to seize the throne for themselves. To prevent any such threat to his power, Amulius decided that the twins must die. Amulius lost no time in carrying out his grim plan. He seized the babies and handed them over to a slave with orders to drown them in the River Tiber. The slave reluctantly put the twins in a basket and placed it in the river.

When the slave reported back to Amulius, the king was pleased – there was now no threat to his throne. However, Amulius was wrong. The children had not drowned, but had been washed ashore, where a she-wolf found them and suckled them. Some time later, a shepherd called Faustulus heard the babies crying and, when he went to investigate, he discovered the wolf feeding them. Astonished, he picked up the twins and took them home to his wife, Larentia.

Faustulus and his wife brought the twins up as their own sons and the boys grew into fine young men. They had no idea who their real parents were until, one day, Remus was captured by robbers. The bandits handed Remus over to Numitor, who was still living in exile. When Romulus heard that his brother had been captured, he immediately set off to rescue him. Both boys now appeared before Numitor who was sure that they must be his long-lost grandsons. Numitor questioned them closely and

This Etruscan bronze statue of a wolf is thought to date from the 5th century BC, but the statues of Romulus and Remus were added in the 15th century AD

then revealed that he was their grandfather. Weeping with joy, the three embraced each other and then made plans to take revenge on Amulius. Within a few days, they had killed Amulius, and Numitor was restored to the throne of Alba Longa.

Numitor was eager for the twins to help him rule Alba Longa, but Romulus and Remus wanted to found a new city. The difficulty was deciding who was to be king. The brothers could not decide the kingship by age as they did not know which of them was the elder twin. Therefore, they decided to look for a sign from the gods. Early societies often believed that the flight of birds revealed the wishes of the gods. So the twins each chose a hill, climbed up it and watched the sky closely. Soon Remus, on the Aventine Hill, saw six eagles (or, in some versions, vultures). His supporters cheered, thinking that Remus would become king. But then Romulus, on the Palatine Hill, saw twelve eagles. His followers, too, rejoiced. It was clear that each twin could claim the kingship – Remus, because he had seen the eagles first, and Romulus, because he had seen more. But Romulus's claim prevailed.

Romulus carefully marked out the plan of his new city and ordered that the whole area be surrounded by city walls. While the walls were still only half-built, Remus visited the building site, eager to discover how the city was progressing. Romulus greeted Remus in a friendly fashion, but Remus taunted Romulus about the size of the city walls. 'What sort of city do you call this, when I can leap over its defences?'

he shouted as he jumped over the walls. Romulus was furious at this insult to his city and, seizing his sword, he killed his brother. As he thrust his sword into Remus's guts, he declared, 'So perish all those who cross my walls.' The city was named Rome after Romulus, who became the first king of Rome. Thus, the ancient Romans believed that, if a she-wolf had not saved an abandoned baby called Romulus, Rome would never have been founded.

After the death of Romulus, Rome continued to be ruled by kings. The seventh king, Tarquin the Proud (Tarquinius Superbus), was the last king of Rome. Tarquin's son, Sextus, raped a woman named Lucretia and a mob of angry citizens resolved to punish him and his family. In the rebellion, Sextus was put to death and Tarquin fled north to Etruria. Tarquin asked the Etruscan king Lars Porsena to help him to retake his throne.

5.2 Horatius Cocles (506 BC)

The Etruscans lived in Etruria, to the north of Rome. In 506 BC, the king of the Etruscan town of Clusium was Lars Porsena. Porsena could see that Rome was becoming increasingly powerful and he was frightened that the Romans would soon threaten his authority. Porsena wanted to curb Rome's power and an excellent opportunity arose when Tarquin the Proud was expelled from Rome. Tarquin asked Porsena to help him to attack Rome and regain his throne. Porsena readily agreed and marched on Rome at the head of a great army.

The road from Etruria to Rome entered the city across a bridge over the River Tiber. This bridge was defended by a fortified hill, the Janiculum Hill, and the Romans had stationed a defensive force on both the bridge and the hill.

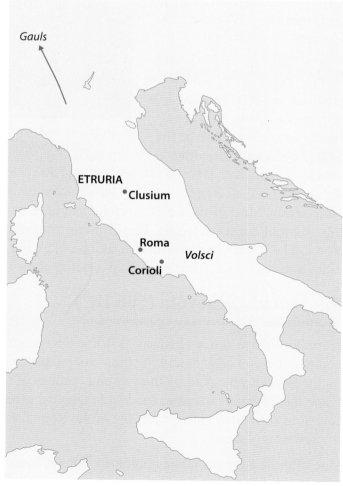

Map of Rome and the surrounding area

However, when the Roman defenders saw the size of the Etruscan army, they fled in terror across the bridge. Their panic-stricken flight left the bridge undefended and there was nothing to prevent the Etruscans marching into Rome.

Rome was in great danger, but a soldier named Horatius Cocles acted swiftly. He knew that the bridge over the River Tiber was so narrow that only a few men could cross it at a time. Horatius bravely rushed onto the middle of the bridge, followed by two friends called Spurius Lartius and Titus Herminius. The three soldiers blocked the bridge and the Etruscan attack was halted. Horatius ordered the Romans to

destroy the bridge from the Roman side, while he and his two comrades held off the attacking Etruscans. The Romans hacked away at the bridge supports and, when the supports were nearly cut through, Horatius told Lartius and Herminius to retreat. Horatius covered their withdrawal and they reached the Roman riverbank safely.

Horatius and his two comrades held off an entire army on the bridge, shown in this 16th century painting

Horatius himself was now in a hopeless position, unable to retreat or advance. Just as the bridge collapsed, Horatius prayed to the River Tiber to protect him and threw himself into the water. The Etruscans fired a hail of arrows at Horatius, but he managed to swim to the Roman bank safely. Most of the Etruscans who had been on the bridge drowned and the others could not reach Rome. The Etruscan attack was halted; Horatius had saved Rome. The Romans hailed Horatius as a hero, giving him as much land as he could plough round in a day and setting up a statue of him in Rome.

5.3 Mucius Scaevola (506 BC)

Horatius's brave actions had saved Rome from immediate defeat, but the Etruscans had no intention of withdrawing their troops. Instead, Porsena increased the pressure on the Romans, blockading the city and cutting off food supplies. Porsena hoped that when the Romans ran out of food and faced the prospect of starvation they would be forced to surrender. However, some of the Romans decided to take immediate action to prevent any such risk.

One of these Romans was a nobleman called Gaius Mucius. Mucius devised a daring plan to kill King Porsena. He hid a dagger under his cloak, slipped out of Rome unobserved and sneaked into the Etruscan camp. By chance, it was payday for the army and the royal paymaster and King Porsena were sitting together. Mucius did not know what Porsena looked like and he mistook the paymaster for the king, since he was splendidly dressed and surrounded by piles of money. Mucius marched forward boldly and, before anyone could stop him, struck down the paymaster with a single blow. Mucius tried to escape, but he was overwhelmed by the guards and dragged before King Porsena.

Porsena was very angry that Mucius had killed one of his servants and he threatened Mucius with all kinds of hideous tortures. Mucius showed no fear, but informed Porsena that he was ready to die bravely, just like any other Roman. He went on: 'Moreover, King, even if you put me to death, there are many other Romans who have sworn to kill you. Eventually one of them will succeed.'

Porsena was infuriated, but he was also concerned about the threat to his life. He ordered that Mucius be burnt alive unless he revealed the whole of the plot to kill him. Mucius was determined to show Porsena that he was not afraid of death, however hideous a form it took, and thrust his right hand into a fire which was burning on a nearby altar. The king was so impressed by Mucius's bravery that he released him and sent him back to Rome, ordering him to report that the Etruscan king was eager to agree peace terms with the Romans. When Mucius returned home, he was given the nickname Scaevola, which means 'left-handed'. Mucius was called this because he had voluntarily destroyed his right hand in the service of Rome.

In this 15th century oil painting, Mucius puts his hands in fire to show Porsena that no Roman feared him

5.4 Cloelia (506 BC)

When the Romans and the Etruscans eventually agreed to make peace, the Etruscan king wanted guarantees that the Romans would not resume the war. Therefore, Porsena demanded that the Romans hand over hostages to him. 'If you break the terms of the peace treaty,' he warned the Romans, 'I shall kill the hostages.'

Many of the hostages came from important Roman families; one of them was a young noblewoman called Cloelia. Cloelia hated being held captive in the Etruscan camp and she resolved to escape. She gathered a group of the hostages and, one night, the women slipped out of their tents, evaded the guards and made for the River Tiber. Then they jumped into the water and struck out for the other bank. Alerted by the noise, the Etruscan guards fired arrows at the women, but the fugitives managed to swim across unharmed. Cloelia then led the group back to Rome and reunited them with their families.

Although the women were delighted to be back in Rome, the Romans were worried that Porsena would be angry at their escape. The Romans were correct to be concerned – Porsena was exceedingly annoyed and said that, if the leader of the escaped hostages did not return, he would resume the war. When Cloelia was told of Porsena's demand she agreed to return to the Etruscan camp, even though she knew that Porsena might kill her. She thought that Rome was more important than she was and wanted to save Rome from another war.

When Porsena realised that Cloelia had returned of her own free will to his camp, he was deeply impressed. He admired Cloelia's bravery and decided to release her. 'You are both bold and patriotic,' Porsena told Cloelia, 'and I am happy to reward so brave a girl as you. I shall let you take some of the remaining hostages back to Rome with you – choose which ones you want.' Cloelia thought carefully about whom to free and eventually decided to take the young boys, as they would grow up to be warriors, whereas the older women could not fight for Rome.

The Romans welcomed Cloelia's second return with great rejoicing. Although statues were rarely raised to honour women, they decided to commemorate Cloelia's bravery by setting up a statue of her riding a horse. This was a great compliment and the Romans placed the statue on an important road called the Sacred Way where many people would see it.

5.5 Coriolanus (493–491 BC)

As Rome continued to expand its power, it increasingly came into conflict with other tribes. At the beginning of the fifth century BC, the Romans were fighting a war against the Volsci, a tribe who lived about thirty miles (fifty kilometres) south east of Rome. The Romans were besieging the Volscian city of Corioli when the Volsci sent reinforcements to attack the Roman troops from the rear. The Romans were in danger of being encircled, but a brave soldier called Gnaeus Marcius acted swiftly. He forced his way inside the walls of Corioli and threw a burning torch into the crowded part of the city. The Volscian crowd panicked and fled from the flames. Without a proper defence, the town soon fell to the Romans. The Romans knew that Marcius's bold actions had led to the capture of Corioli and they called him Coriolanus – conqueror of Corioli – in recognition of his bravery.

After the war, Coriolanus became involved in Roman politics. At this point, there was considerable political rivalry between the patricians (who were powerful, wealthy people) and the plebeians (the ordinary people). The leaders of the plebeians were growing more influential and they insisted that food ought to be sold cheaply, so that everyone could afford it. Coriolanus disliked the plebeians and he arrogantly opposed their leaders' wishes. Soon the war hero Coriolanus had become so unpopular that he was expelled from Rome and he went to live with the Volsci, who were now at peace with the Romans.

Coriolanus was very angry about how he had been treated and he wanted revenge. The Volsci greatly respected Coriolanus's courage and, although they were at peace with Rome, many of the Volsci listened to Coriolanus as he continually urged them to attack Rome once more. One of Coriolanus's close friends was a Volscian called Attius Tullius and the two devised a plan to bring about war.

The Romans were celebrating some important festival games and many Volsci had gone to Rome to watch the games. Tullius, pretending to be an ally of the Romans, warned leading Roman officials that the visiting Volsci might attack Rome. The Romans remembered that they had recently been fighting the Volsci and decided to expel them from Rome as a precaution against a sudden attack. The Volsci were infuriated at this insult and, as Coriolanus and Tullius had planned, they declared war on Rome.

The Volsci appointed Coriolanus commander of the Volscian army and he soon demonstrated his skill, capturing many towns. The Roman Senate was deeply concerned about Coriolanus's victories and sent envoys and priests to beg for mercy. Coriolanus dismissed them with utter contempt. No argument could persuade Coriolanus, no army could defeat him – it seemed as if Rome itself must soon fall to the Volsci. In despair, the women of Rome approached Coriolanus's mother Veturia and his wife Volumnia. 'We have tried everything else,' they pleaded. 'Rome will fall unless you help us.' Veturia agreed with them and set off towards the Volsci camp outside the gates of Rome, accompanied by Coriolanus's wife and two small sons. Coriolanus was delighted to see his family again and rushed forward to meet them. However, his mother would not embrace him – 'You are no son of mine if you attack the city of your fathers,' she proclaimed. Coriolanus was deeply moved by her words and withdrew from Rome.

The Volsci were, not surprisingly, extremely angry that Coriolanus had betrayed their cause. Some versions of the legend say that the Volsci drove Coriolanus into exile, but others record that the Volsci put him to death to punish him for his unfaithfulness.

5.6 Manlius Torquatus (361 BC and 340 BC)

The Gauls were a warlike people who lived far to the north of Rome. By the fourth century BC, the Romans and the Gauls had come into conflict. The Gauls posed a considerable threat to Roman expansion.

Around 361 BC, the Gauls had come within three miles (five kilometres) of Rome. The two sides clashed at a river crossing and the troops fought to a standstill. While both sides rested, a huge Gaul stepped forward and proposed a solution to the stalemate. He challenged any Roman to fight him in single combat and said that whoever won would control the ford. The Romans noted the Gaul's great size and the sharp blades of his weapons; at first no one wanted to fight him, but eventually a soldier named Titus Manlius volunteered. Manlius fought bravely and soon defeated the Gaul. He brandished the Gaul's weapons in the air and took his torque from his body. A torque was a heavy gold collar worn round the neck and the Romans now called Manlius 'Torquatus' in commemoration of his spectacular victory.

Only Manlius was brave enough to fight the huge Gaul in single combat

Over the following years, Manlius continued to be a successful soldier and he gained considerable political power, becoming consul three times. (Rome was ruled by two consuls who held office for one year at a time.) However, tragedy struck in 340 BC when his son was serving alongside him. At this point, Rome was fighting a tribe called the Latins. Young Manlius was in charge of a small group of soldiers who had been told to reconnoitre the ground, but had been ordered not to become involved in actual fighting. Unfortunately, while young Manlius was carrying out his reconnaissance, he was spotted by a group of Latins. One of the Latins, called Geminus Metius, taunted young Manlius. 'Are you Romans all such cowards that you run away from your enemy?' shouted the Latin. 'Why don't you come over here and fight?' Young Manlius felt that he could not ignore such an insult and, determined to show that he did not lack courage, he challenged Metius to fight in single combat.

Young Manlius easily overcame the Latin and took his weapons from his body. No Romans had been lost in the confrontation and Manlius returned in triumph to the Roman camp. He proudly laid his spoils before his father, but Torquatus did not praise his son for a deed similar to what he himself had done in his youth. Instead, he turned to him and spoke sternly: 'You were ordered not to fight. You have disobeyed both the standing military orders of a consul and the command of your own father. If I do not punish you, all discipline will be lost in the army.'

Torquatus then summoned guards, who led young Manlius out to the courtyard. The young man was tied to a stake and a guard cut off his head with a single blow from an axe. In this brutal way, Manlius Torquatus ensured that military discipline was maintained within the army.

Exercise 5.1

1. (a) Tell the story of the birth and childhood of Romulus and Remus.
   (b) Do you think that Amulius had any justification for his actions? Explain why you think this.
2. (a) Describe how the city of Rome came to be founded.
   (b) If you had been Romulus, how would you have dealt with Remus and why?
3. (a) Tell the story of Romulus and Remus from the viewpoint of Numitor.
   (b) Do you think that Numitor would have believed that Romulus would make a good king? Explain your answer.

Extension work

Write an essay considering why you think that Romans liked to tell the story of Romulus and Remus and other stories about Roman heroes. What might Romans have felt that they could learn from such tales?

Exercise 5.2

1. (a) Tell the story of Horatius and the bridge.
   (b) Why do you think that the Romans admired Horatius so much?
2. (a) What happened to Mucius Scaevola?
   (b) What qualities did Mucius Scaevola demonstrate? Explain your answer.
3. (a) Horatius and Mucius both tried to defend Rome from Porsena. Explain what they did.
   (b) Which of the two do you consider to have been more brave and why do you think this?

Extension work

In your capacity as a top Hollywood film producer, draw the film stills for the battle scene from your new production about Horatius. You will need to illustrate the arrival of the Etruscan army, the Roman army in flight, Horatius and his two friends, and his escape from the bridge.

Exercise 5.3

1. (a) How did Cloelia come to be a hostage? What did she do about it?
   (b) Most of the stories of early Rome are about men, not women. Why do you think this is the case?
2. (a) Tell the story of Coriolanus.
   (b) What do you most admire about Coriolanus and what do you least admire about him?
3. (a) Assess the actions of Cloelia and Veturia, the mother of Coriolanus.
   (b) Do you think they were particularly brave, considering that they were women?

Extension work

Many of the legends of early Rome are about men. However, women such as Cloelia and Veturia were also celebrated. Research more examples of legendary women from the early history of Rome (such as Lucretia, Verginia or the Sabine Women) and assess what qualities these women showed.

Exercise 5.4

1. (a) Tell the story of how Manlius gained his early fame.
   (b) Do you think that giving Manlius a nickname was a worthwhile reward? Why do you think this?
2. (a) Explain what happened to Titus Manlius's son.
   (b) How would you have dealt with young Manlius and why would you have done this?
3. (a) Both Romulus and Torquatus killed a close relative. Explain what they did.
   (b) Explain which of the two you feel was more justified in his actions.

Extension work

Young Manlius is to be tried by a military court martial. Write the main speech for EITHER the prosecution OR the defence, exploring what he did and what should happen to him. Deliver your speech to your class and try to convince them to vote in your favour.

CHAPTER 6 ROMAN ENTERTAINMENT

In the previous chapter we learnt about the early history of Rome, and how it grew up from the small town founded by Romulus into a city capable of defeating its enemies across Italy. As it became more powerful, so its population grew and the ever-increasing number of citizens needed to be entertained.

Public entertainment was an important part of life in Ancient Rome. Baths were open daily and Romans visited bath complexes as much for the opportunity to meet each other as to get clean. Theatres provided a variety of different types of entertainment, from serious drama to slapstick mime. Gladiatorial games and chariot racing were hugely popular and took place regularly during public holidays, which were extremely frequent. Indeed, by the first century AD there were 159 holidays per year, 93 of which had public games.

The various forms of public entertainment were so important to the Romans that wealthy men often spent considerable sums of money covering the costs of state entertainment. For example, when the politician Agrippa was the **aedile** (a type of magistrate) in charge of public buildings, he paid for everyone to visit the baths free of charge. Such men hoped that their generosity would win them popularity and votes in elections.

6.1 The theatre

At the theatre

The first Roman theatres had been made of wood, but the Romans soon began to build permanent structures in stone. The basic design of Roman theatres shares similarities with modern theatre buildings. There was a semi-circular stage, with rows of seats rising in tiers to a top storey. At the back of the stage, there was a structure called the *scaena*. The *scaena* was two or three storeys high and had various different stage entrances. These entrances were particularly useful for suggesting that actors had come from different parts of a house or a street. Characters could also use the upper storeys and appear in upstairs windows.

Although the word *scaena* gives us the English word 'scene', there was very little scenery in Roman theatres. The stage buildings were occasionally painted, but Roman theatres were far too large for detailed backdrops such as are used today in modern theatres. For example, Marcellus (who was the nephew of the Emperor Augustus) built a theatre with 12,000 seats and the Theatre of Pompey had 40,000. If scenery were used, it was generally designed to look like a street scene. Revolving scenery was sometimes used and the Romans had an impressive mechanical crane, which hoisted actors across the stage as if they were flying. This crane was most often used to transport actors playing gods and has come to be called the **deus ex machina** ('the god from the machine').

Roman theatres were open to the air, but, if it were hot, awnings (*velaria*) could be drawn over the roof of the theatre. Between performances, attendants also sprinkled perfumed water to cool the theatre.

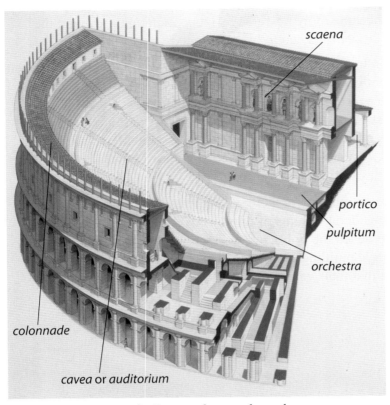

This reconstruction of a Roman theatre shows how well built the theatres were

While the front seats were reserved for senators (important politicians) and prestigious guests, entry to the theatre was free because important citizens or the Emperor covered the costs of a performance. Performances could last for several hours and audience members came prepared. They brought cushions to make the stone seats more comfortable and they also carried food and drink. Not all of this food was to eat: Roman audiences were difficult to please and some spectators brought rotten fruit to throw at bad actors! If members of the audience did not like an actor or a play, they would walk out or shout at the actors. Bad actors were sometimes hissed off the stage.

Roman actors wore masks, which may have helped to project the voice. More importantly, masks were easy to recognise at a distance because they were of a standard pattern. Male characters wore brown masks, while female characters had white masks. There were other conventions: old men had white hair and beards, slaves wore red wigs and women had long hair. As a result, audiences had no difficulty in identifying who was who, even if they were sitting far away from the stage. Roman theatres also had excellent acoustics, which enabled every word to be heard clearly.

Plays and playwrights

The Greeks had invented drama and Roman theatre was greatly influenced by Greek elements. Plays by the three great Greek writers of tragedy (Aeschylus, Sophocles

and Euripides) were still performed in Rome, centuries after they were written. Although Roman authors also wrote tragedies, these were often based on Greek myths.

The main Roman playwrights were Terence and Plautus, who wrote comedies, and Seneca, who wrote serious plays. The Roman public preferred comedies. Many Roman comedies were based on Greek originals, so the characters had Greek names and wore Greek clothes. A typical plot would involve a young man in love with a beautiful girl. Normally, the young man's father would disapprove of the romance, because the girl was either very poor or a slave. A cheeky, but loyal, slave would help his young master to trick his father. The girl often turned out to be a rich man's daughter who had been lost or kidnapped when young. Finally, everything ended happily with the young man and girl marrying.

The Romans also enjoyed other types of plays, including farce, mime and pantomime. Farce had originated as comic performances that mocked provincial Italian life. Early farces were acted by amateurs, but from the first century BC professionals took over.

Mime was performed by professional actors, including women. The performances consisted of short scenes of city life, in which both ordinary events and politics were caricatured. Unlike modern mime, Roman mime could include some dialogue. Mime was generally crude – blasphemy, sex and violence were key ingredients. Occasionally, ruthless emperors, such as the Emperor Domitian (81–96 AD), ordered that a condemned criminal take the place of an actor – the criminal would then die the death that was normally acted out on stage by an actor.

Pantomime appealed to a more sophisticated audience than mime. However, Roman pantomime was significantly different from modern pantomime,

In this mosaic from the 1st century AD you can see actors preparing for a performance. Note the masks and musical instruments

being a kind of ballet with a musical accompaniment of flutes, cymbals, trumpets and castanets. Pantomimes were based on mythological themes (which were usually serious) and the words were sung, rather than spoken. Often there was only one main actor (the word pantomime means 'acting everything'), accompanied by a choir. Top pantomime singers or dancers could become immensely popular.

Despite the variety of entertainment on offer, the Romans were less enthusiastic about the theatre than the Greeks. Visiting the theatre was significantly less popular than visiting the races or the amphitheatre.

6.2 The amphitheatre

Two of the most popular forms of Roman entertainment were gladiatorial shows and wild-beast hunts. These events took place in amphitheatres, which were oval or circular structures with banked rows of seats looking down onto a sandy arena. Amphitheatres were found across the Roman world, but the most impressive amphitheatre was the **Colosseum** in Rome. This vast building measured 3,500 square metres and could hold 50,000 people (45,000 sitting and 5,000 standing). The Colosseum had 80 separate entrances so that the huge crowd could enter easily. The different entrances were numbered; all the spectators had to do was to match up the number on their ticket (*tessera*) with the number on the entrance and then look for a spare seat.

The Emperor had his own imperial box (*pulvinar*) with a special underground exit. The best seats near ground level were reserved for senators and the rows behind were

This reconstruction of the Colosseum shows the careful design which made it large enough to hold 50,000 people

kept for the *equites* (knights). Ordinary men sat in the remaining rows while women sat in the top rows. Slaves were admitted to the standing room on the terrace as long as there were spare places. If it rained, or there was excessive sunshine, an enormous awning was winched into place to protect the audience.

The costs of the games were paid for either by the Emperor or by ambitious magistrates who wanted to gain popularity with the ordinary people. Each show began with a grand parade – the gladiators wore purple cloaks embroidered with gold and they walked, or drove in chariots, round the arena to the accompaniment of music. When the gladiators reached the Emperor's box they greeted him with the phrase *ave Caesar, morituri te salutant* – 'Hail Caesar, those who are about to die salute you'.

Gladiators were normally slaves (often prisoners-of-war) who were chosen for their toughness and physique. The training regime was demanding and many men died before reaching the arena. Criminals might become gladiators as an alternative to deportation or being sentenced to work in the mines. However, this only applied to those who had been convicted of lesser offences. Most criminals who ended up in the arena were those who were condemned to be killed by wild beasts. Occasionally, very poor citizens opted to become gladiators

This Roman mosaic shows an official supervising a fight between two gladiators

because they had no money. However, this was a rare form of recruitment.

There were four basic types of gladiators: Samnite, Gaul, Thracian and *Retiarius*. The first three were 'pursuers' (*secutores*), or more attacking gladiators. The Samnite was the most heavily armed gladiator – he carried a large rectangular shield and a short sword or axe. Additionally, a Samnite wore a helmet with a visor, a breastplate and greaves (metal leg-guards) on his arms and legs. The Gaul (who was often called a *murmillo*) also had a large rectangular shield, breastplate, greaves and a sword. He was distinguished from a Samnite by the picture of a fish or other sea creature on his helmet. The Thracian was less heavily armed. He carried a sword (which was often curved) and a light, round shield, which was much smaller than the shield of a Samnite. Although the Thracian wore a breastplate, he did not always wear a helmet

Gaul

Samnite

Retiarius

Gauls and Samnites were much more heavily armed than
Retiarii, *who normally had no protection*

and he was not protected by leg or arm greaves. The *Retiarius* had no protective armour, but carried a three-pronged trident, a dagger and a net. The *Retiarius* relied on his quickness of movement to catch his opponent in the net and then spear him with his trident. Occasionally, gladiators might fight from chariots or from horseback and there were even some female gladiators.

While each type of gladiator might fight against a similar type (for example, two Samnites pitted against each other), Roman audiences particularly enjoyed watching the heavily armed *secutores* being matched against the more nimble *Retiarii*. Such a pairing resulted in a contest between brute force and agility.

Death, freedom and spectacle

Roman audiences were bloodthirsty – they wanted to see exciting fights and they enjoyed watching people die in front of them. Individual gladiators who pleased the crowd by their bravery or personality could become immensely popular and many Romans bet on the outcome of fights, although this was illegal. The atmosphere at the Colosseum was often electrifying, just as at some modern sporting events. The noise of excited supporters cheering on their favourites could change to a shocked hush as a gladiator took a bad hit; roars of approval for a good recovery could turn to loud booing if a fighter appeared to be cowardly or if there was an unpopular decision by the president of the games.

Although many modern sportsmen are passionate about winning, they do not face the prospect of death if they lose. Roman gladiators did. They were literally fighting for their lives. Victory brought money and a crown, but a defeated gladiator was either killed outright or left lying on the sand, making a final, desperate appeal to the crowd to be spared. If the spectators thought he had fought well they would wave their handkerchiefs or give a signal with their thumbs. Some accounts suggest that a 'thumbs down' meant that the sword was to be returned to its scabbard and the gladiator was to be spared, whereas a 'thumbs up' meant that the sword was to be driven into his throat and he was to be put to death. Other people think that a 'thumbs down' was the sign for death. Whichever signal was used, the president of the games (often the Emperor) normally accepted the crowd's wishes. If the gladiator were spared, he was allowed to rise and leave the arena. If the crowd rejected the appeal, the defeated gladiator was put to death amid a fanfare of trumpets. His body was dragged off by attendants dressed as the messengers of the Underworld, and fresh sand (*harena*) was scattered where his blood had fallen. By midday, the smell of blood was so great that perfume was sprinkled on the crowd and incense was burned to try to cover up the stench.

Some gladiators managed to save enough money to buy their freedom. However, most gladiators only earned their freedom after years of successful fighting. A freed gladiator was given a wooden sword (*rudis*), the sign that the gladiator could retire from the arena. An ex-gladiator might become a trainer (*lanista*) in a gladiatorial training school. However, some gladiators returned to the arena after receiving their freedom either because they needed the money (many had no other training) or because they missed the excitement and the prestige that their victories brought them. Romans turned some of their gladiators into celebrities: graffiti from Pompeii shows that individual gladiators could become immensely popular with both men and women – some women even claimed to have fallen in love with them!

Gladiators were costly to train and organisers did not want to lose too many gladiators in a show. Condemned criminals, on the other hand, cost nothing and could be executed in a variety of imaginative ways – often in the lunchtime break between the main gladiatorial contests. Criminals might be forced to take the part of some ill-fated mythological person (such as Actaeon, who was torn apart by hounds). However, the most common method of putting criminals to death was to condemn them to be killed by wild beasts, such as lions, tigers, wild dogs or bears. Criminals might be chained or nailed to stakes, but were often left to run free as this gave added excitement. The animals that killed the criminals had often been starved for several days to ensure that their hunger overcame their fear of men and the unknown arena.

Animals were also used in wild-beast hunts (***venationes***). Sometimes one type of animal (***bestia***) was set against another. For example, a pack of wild dogs might face a single lion. Alternatively, animals were matched against men known as ***Bestiarii*** (beast fighters). *Bestiarii* fought with a variety of weapons. The most common was a long spear, but *Bestiarii* also used clubs or bows and arrows. *Bestiarii* might fight a single beast or tackle a group of animals. The more obscure the animal, the more popular the contest – giraffes, elephants and hippopotami all featured in wild-beast hunts. Lions, tigers and leopards were used so often that they became much rarer – the Roman author Cicero wrote from Asia Minor joking that the local supply of panthers had run out owing to demands from the amphitheatre! Certainly, very large numbers of animals were regularly slaughtered to satisfy the Romans' lust for blood: 5,000 wild beasts were killed in one day to celebrate the opening of the Colosseum in 80 AD.

Very rarely, the Roman public was entertained with mock sea battles (***naumachiae***). These took place either in man-made lakes near the River Tiber or in Rome itself at the Colosseum. It was easy to get a supply of water near the Tiber, but if the Colosseum were used, it had to be waterproofed and flooded with water from aqueducts. In the mock sea battles, gladiators and slaves manned small, fast ships with many oars. The aim was to defeat all the other ships, and those who fought exceptionally bravely might be freed. Mock battles were extremely popular, but were rarely staged because of the huge cost and amount of preparation involved.

6.3 Chariot racing

The Circus Maximus

Just as gladiatorial shows spread throughout the Roman Empire, so did chariot racing. Racetracks could be found in cities as far apart as Alexandria and Constantinople, and there were three racetracks within Rome itself. The oldest and most famous chariot-racing track was the **Circus Maximus** in Rome. The Circus Maximus was remodelled over time and, by the reign of the Emperor Trajan (98–117 AD), it had three tiers of seats which held between 200,000 and 255,000 people. Entry to the Circus Maximus was free and, unlike in amphitheatres, men, women and children were allowed to sit together.

The course consisted of an oval track around a central barrier or ***spina*** (literally, the backbone). Chariots raced round the track in an anti-clockwise direction. At the end of each straight, the track curved tightly around the end of the *spina*. These curved sections were marked by three bronze turning posts (***metae***) on the *spina*. There were normally twenty-four races in a day and most races had seven laps. A seven lap race was about 7 to 8 kilometres and lasted around fifteen minutes. At each end of the *spina* there was a lap counter, which consisted of seven large wooden eggs (***ova***). One egg (***ovum***) was removed at the end of each lap so that spectators could see how many were left. Later, bronze dolphins were also used as lap counters.

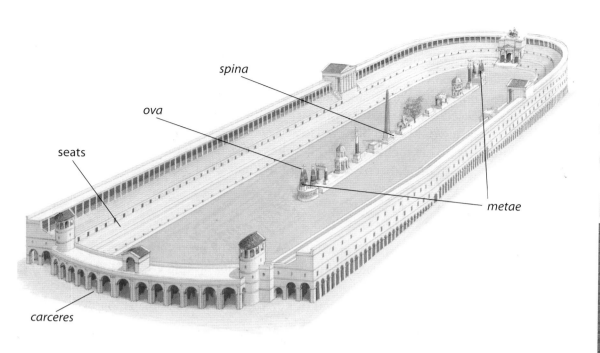

An artist's impression of the Circus Maximus in Rome

Usually, four horses were harnessed to a chariot (the **quadriga**, or four-horsed chariot). Sometimes two, three, six or eight horses were used, although chariots drawn by more than four horses were difficult to control. Occasionally trick races were put on: for example, trick riders (**desultores**), who controlled two single horses without chariots, jumped between them in mid-race.

For most of Rome's history there were four different chariot teams (**factiones**). These were the Reds (**Russati**), Blues (**Veneti**), Whites (**Albati**) and Greens (**Prasini**). The Emperor Domitian (81–96 AD) introduced two new teams, Purple and Gold, but this novelty did not last long. Each racing team had its own stables, trainers, horses and fanatical supporters. Like modern football supporters, chariot-racing fans were devoted to their teams and wore their team colours to matches. Fans bet heavily on the result (although this was illegal) and could get involved in fights with rival supporters. Chariot racing was very popular with all parts of Roman society, from the poorest to the Emperor himself: the Emperor Nero (54–68 AD) even took part in one race in the Circus Maximus. Fans loyally supported successful charioteers (**agitatores** or **aurigae**) and even individual horses might gain great popularity. The Emperor Caligula (37–41 AD) was a fanatical follower of the Greens and he liked one horse, called Incitatus, so much that he gave it a marble stall, purple blankets and jewels. Caligula was even rumoured to have wanted to make it consul!

The atmosphere at the Circus Maximus would have been similar to that at an important modern sports fixture today. There would have been vast numbers

(200,000–250,000) of eager supporters wearing their team's colours, pushing through the crowds trying to find their seats. Busy groups of slaves and free men – drivers, vets, stable hands and managers – would have stood around the horses, trying to ensure the best possible conditions and results. There would have been tradesmen selling hot food, drinks and souvenirs of the event. Finally, there would have been harassed officials attempting to start the event on time with no mistakes. Everywhere there would have been noise and shouting – sellers calling out prices, men making bets, excited children and families cheering on their team and the odd cry of protest as someone discovered that a thief had taken advantage of the tumult to steal his purse …

A day at the races

A day at the races began with the starting procession. Trumpeters and flute players played music while the charioteers slowly drove their chariots around the track. Soldiers marched behind the chariots, carrying images of the gods. These images often included Neptune, the patron god of horses; Jupiter, the king of the gods; Mars, the god of war and Venus, the goddess of love.

When the starting procession was over, it was time to begin the races. Twelve teams of horses were coaxed into the starting boxes (*carceres*) and then the presiding magistrate, who was often the Emperor, took charge. He held a white cloth (*mappa*) high up in his hand – when he dropped it, this was the signal (*signum*) for the start.

In this artist's impression, a charioteer urges on his horses.
Many charioteers died or were maimed for life following crashes

Then the teams leapt out of the starting boxes, each jostling for a good position on the track.

The most dangerous and exciting part of the course lay in the tight turn around the **metae**, or turning posts. The *metae* consisted of three cones of gilded bronze mounted on the *spina*. Chariots had to slow down to make the turn, but charioteers normally tried to keep to the inside of the track. While the outer section of the curve gave more room for manoeuvre, it also took longer to cover and another chariot might overtake on the inside. Following a tight curve close to the *metae* gave the shortest route, but there was the danger of driving too quickly and losing control. Moreover, since most charioteers chose this inner route, it was easy to crash into other chariots. Most crashes occurred at the *metae*, especially when chariots were deliberately forced into the walls by their rivals. Crashes could easily be fatal, particularly as charioteers drove with the reins tied round their bodies for greater support when standing upright in unstable chariots. Charioteers knew the risk of being caught in the reins and dragged to their deaths, so they carried knives to cut themselves free if they crashed.

A successful charioteer could make a lot of money but many charioteers died young or suffered terrible injuries in accidents. Most charioteers were slaves who hoped to earn enough money to buy their freedom. However, one of the most successful charioteers was a Spaniard called Diocles who retired in 150 AD. In the course of a twenty-four year career, he took part in 4,257 races, winning 1,462 and earning nearly 36 million *sestertii*. Other successful charioteers also gained high rewards; for example, the Emperor Caligula gave Eutychus, who drove for the Greens, 2 million *sestertii*. (A loaf of bread at this time would be half a *sestertius*.)

Not everyone enjoyed the races. The Roman writer Pliny the Younger complained about the dullness of chariot racing in a letter:

> There is nothing new or different about them, one race is enough. So I am all the more surprised that so many thousands of men have so childish a desire as to watch, again and again, horses running and men standing in chariots. If they were drawn by the speed of the horses or the skill of the men, there would be a reason, but, in fact, it is a little bit of cloth which they support. If the racing-colours were transferred from one chariot to another in the middle of a race, the supporters would transfer their enthusiasm and suddenly abandon those horses and drivers whose names they keep shouting.
>
> Pliny, Letters 9.6

6.4 The baths

Visiting the baths was a popular and pleasant part of Roman daily life. There were many bath complexes (*balneae* or *thermae*) throughout the Roman Empire, from Scotland to North Africa, and the English city of Bath takes its name from its Roman baths. Bath complexes were very popular in Rome, too, and by the third century AD there were over one thousand bath-houses in Rome. Some were very small; others, such as the 27 acre Baths of Caracalla, were magnificent structures, built in expensive marble and decorated with lavish mosaics.

Design and layout

Although baths varied considerably in size and luxuriousness, most followed a similar basic layout.

Going to the baths was a chance to socialise or meet business contacts as well as to get clean

Some baths, such as those at **Aquae Sulis** (Bath) in Britain, were built around an existing hot spring, but most baths drew their water supply from aqueducts and heated the water using an underground heating system called a **hypocaust**. With a hypocaust, the floor was not laid directly on the ground. A series of piles of bricks was placed on the foundations and the floor was then laid on top of these supports. This meant that there was room for air to circulate under the floor. A charcoal or wood furnace was also built beneath the floor. When lit, the hot air from the furnace circulated under the floor and heated the room above. Sometimes channels were built into the walls to provide additional heating from the side. The hot bath was placed as close to the furnace as possible. If there was more than one hot bath (for example, where there was a men's and a women's bath), then the two would be placed on either side of the furnace.

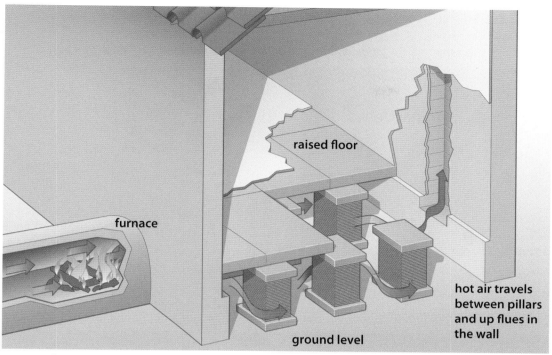

raised floor

furnace

hot air travels
between pillars
and up flues in
the wall

ground level

The hypocaust enabled hot air to flow under the floor, heating the rooms above.
Some hypocausts had channels built into the walls

Baths had special entrances, which varied in magnificence according to the size of
the bath complex. Some entrances were small, while others were grand rooms,
painted with fine decorations. Large bath complexes might have more than one
entrance. Once a bather had entered the bath complex, he would head for the
apodyterium (changing room). Here the bather undressed and left his clothes in a
niche in the wall. Bathers entered the baths naked, although they had a towel with
which to rub themselves down. Thieves regularly haunted bath-houses in the hope of
stealing unguarded clothes, so it was necessary either to leave your own slave
watching your clothes or to pay a bath-house slave to look after them.

After changing, bathers entered the ***tepidarium*** (warm room). Benches ran round the
walls and bathers sat in the steamy atmosphere, talking to each other. The next room
was the ***caldarium*** (hot room), where the air temperature was very high. There was a
large bath filled with hot water where bathers would soak their bodies. When a
bather had finished in the hot water, he emerged and lay down on a marble slab. Now
was the time to clean the body. A slave applied oil (***unguentum***) all over the bather
and massaged the oil into the skin. This oil varied in price; the most costly would
have contained the best quality oil and perfume. Next, the slave scraped off the
excess oil with a curved metal scraper called a ***strigil***. This action removed dirt and
dead skin from the body. The high temperature of the *caldarium* also encouraged the
body to sweat out impurities in the skin. As well as hot water, there was a supply of
cold water that the bather could splash on his body to help him to cool down.

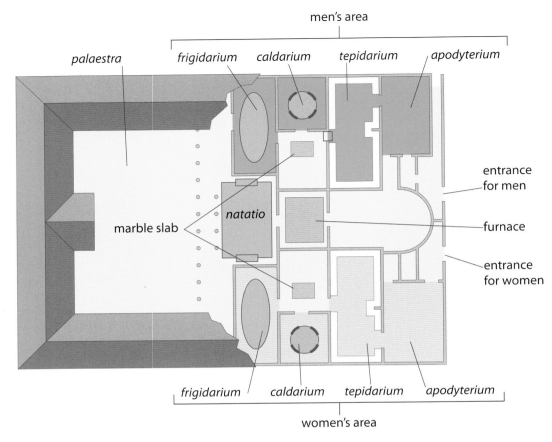

men's area

palaestra   frigidarium   caldarium   tepidarium   apodyterium

natatio

marble slab

entrance for men

furnace

entrance for women

frigidarium   caldarium   tepidarium   apodyterium

women's area

Not all Roman baths had separate areas for men and women; if they did not, women would visit the baths at a different time

Many bathers went from the *caldarium* to the **frigidarium** (cold room). Here there was a deep pool of unheated water and bathers plunged into the pool for a refreshing cold rinse. The bather would then leave the pool, dry off and return to the *apodyterium*. Some bath complexes also had a **natatio** (swimming pool) or a **laconicum** (a room that gave out an intense dry heat, like a modern sauna).

The baths were often decorated with mosaics. Normally, these had a marine theme, with pictures of fish and other sea creatures. Stone (including marble) was used to cover bricks and, in luxurious baths, builders used various costly types of marble, which had different patterns.

As well as the bathing rooms, baths often contained a **palaestra** (exercise ground). This was an open space surrounded by columns. A variety of activities took place here, normally carried out before the actual bath. Ball games were popular, such as **trigon** (a throwing and catching game for three people) or **harpastum** (where the ball was snatched). Men might also wrestle, practise weightlifting or improve their sword skills by fencing at a wooden post.

A typical bath-house

Men, women and children all used the baths. There was no entry charge for children but men and women normally paid a *quadrans* (the smallest coin). Large bath complexes, such as the Stabian Baths at Pompeii, had separate areas for men and women. The women's sections were normally smaller and did not have a *palaestra*. Other baths lacked separate areas for the different sexes so men and women visited at different times. There were also baths that were for men only. Some rich families had their own baths in their houses, although they might also visit public baths to keep up to date with gossip. Baths were so important to the Romans that permanent army camps had baths for the soldiers.

The Romans visited the baths for social reasons as well as to clean themselves and to exercise. Although baths opened in the morning, the most popular time to visit appears to have been in the afternoon. The baths were a great place to meet up with friends, to socialise, to swap gossip and political news, or to have a drink and a snack. Hairdressers and barbers were often available and big bath complexes might include gardens in which to stroll, and libraries. Men even conducted business deals at the baths. Many bath-houses had shops near the entrance which were rented out to different shopkeepers. Some shops sold ordinary goods, while others specifically catered for bath-goers, selling perfumed oil or snacks.

Baths were very busy, popular places. The Roman writer Seneca preserves an impression of the atmosphere at the baths:

'The keep-fit fanatics grunt as they lift their lead weights, they gasp and pant as they exercise … A less active man is having a massage and I hear the slap of the masseur's hand coming down on his shoulders … Then there is a ball-player who shouts out the result, someone starting a fight, a thief being caught, the man who sings in the bath and those who leap into the pool with a huge splash. Finally there is the hair-remover … whose victim cries out, the man selling drink, the sausage-seller and the seller of pastries, each calling out with his own separate cry.'
Seneca, Letter 56

Exercise 6.1

1. (a) Draw and label a detailed plan of a typical Roman theatre. Use Latin as well as English names where possible.
   (b) Name two similarities between the Roman theatre and modern theatre.

ROMANS

63

2. (a) Describe a day out at the Roman theatre. Make sure that you include the seating arrangements, what the stage and actors looked like and what the atmosphere was like.

   (b) Would you prefer to visit the Roman theatre or a modern performance? Explain your answer.

3. (a) Give a detailed description of the different types of plays that you could see in a Roman theatre.

   (b) Which type of play would you most have enjoyed seeing at a Roman theatre and why?

Extension work

Carry out further research into either Greek or Roman drama. Choose a scene from a play and act it out to your class.

Exercise 6.2

1. (a) Describe a day spent at the Colosseum in Roman times.

   (b) Graffiti at Pompeii shows that many people admired gladiators. Do you? Explain your answer.

2. (a) Describe in detail a fight between a typical pair of Roman gladiators.

   (b) Despite the dangers, some freed gladiators did not retire but continued to fight. Give two reasons why this might occur.

3. (a) Various different events occurred in amphitheatres as well as ordinary gladiatorial combat. Describe these different events in detail (do not include normal gladiatorial combat).

   (b) Give two reasons why the Romans found visiting the amphitheatre exciting.

Extension work

Write an essay discussing whether modern forms of entertainment are always superior to Roman forms, or whether some of the more unpleasant aspects of Roman leisure pursuits (brutality, cruelty, etc.) are also reflected in modern entertainment (such as films).

Exercise 6.3

1. (a) Draw a detailed plan of the Circus Maximus, labelling as many features as possible in both Latin and English.

   (b) What resemblances are there between chariot racing and modern sports?

2. (a) Describe the build-up to and preparation for a day's chariot racing at the Circus Maximus.
   What would the atmosphere have been like in the Circus?

   (b) Give two reasons why the Romans found chariot racing exciting.

3. (a) Describe a full day's entertainment at the Circus Maximus.
   (b) Charioteers were often popular figures in Ancient Roman society. Suggest two reasons why this might have been the case.

Extension work

Write the illustrated biography or autobiography of a famous charioteer. Do not forget to explain how he ended up in his profession, as well as what happened to him in it.

Exercise 6.4

1. (a) Draw a detailed diagram showing how Roman baths were heated and write a short description explaining how they were decorated.
   (b) Why do you think that ordinary Romans went to the baths so regularly?
2. (a) Describe an afternoon spent at the baths.
   (b) What would you most enjoy about the Roman baths and what would you least enjoy? Explain your answer.
3. (a) Draw and label (in English and Latin) a plan of a typical Roman bath.
   (b) Why do you think that rich men often paid money for the cost of the upkeep of Roman baths?

Extension work

You are a talented architect attempting to convince a rich Roman that he ought to employ you to build a new bath-house. Decide whether the bath-house is to be public or private and then put together your design package. You should include some of the following: layout, source of water, building materials, sample mosaic patterns, employment of any necessary slaves, exercise equipment, schedule of costs. You may choose to build a model of your bath-house or to present it as drawings.

Exercise 6.5

1. (a) Describe the main points of a day at the amphitheatre and a day at the races.
   (b) Which do you think would have been most exciting to an ancient Roman and why?
2. (a) Describe the various types of plays performed in Roman theatres and the different activities and rooms to be found in Roman bath-houses.
   (b) State which you would rather visit and why.
3. (a) Describe the layout of the *Colosseum* and of a typical Roman theatre.
   (b) Name one similarity and one difference between the two structures.

Extension work

Design an illustrated brochure for the city of Rome in ancient times, giving details of the entertainment on offer to a visitor.

CHAPTER 7 DOMESTIC LIFE

7.1 Roman clothing

Teenagers often claim that wearing the wrong clothes can result in 'social death', but in Roman society, a slave who was caught wearing a woollen garment called a ***toga*** could be literally put to death. The toga was the mark of a citizen. Anyone else who wore it was threatening to overturn the strict structure of Roman society.

The toga was large, heavy and so difficult to put on that rich men often ordered two of their slaves to help them get dressed. First, the toga was wound carefully around the wearer, then the end was passed under the right arm and thrown over the left shoulder. Its semi-circular shape meant the wider centre fell gracefully in loose folds to the feet but, although it was elegant, it was utterly unsuitable for active wear. Moreover, the heavy woollen cloth made the toga inappropriate for hot weather. Most Roman men wore the toga only at formal occasions.

Different varieties of toga also revealed the ranks of Roman society. Ordinary men wore a plain creamy-white toga called the ***toga virilis*** or the ***toga pura***. Important officials, such as magistrates, priests and senators, as well as boys under sixteen, wore the ***toga praetexta*** (white with a broad purple stripe).

Romans also distinguished between various social groups by the colour of their tunics. The ***tunica*** was rather like a long t-shirt and was often sleeveless. It reached down to just above the knee and was worn belted around the waist. Only senators might wear the ***tunica laticlavia***, which was white, with a broad purple stripe down the front. The less important *equites* wore white tunics with two narrow purple stripes running down the front of the tunic on either side of the neck. Everyone else wore ordinary tunics, which varied in terms of quality, colours and patterns. The cheapest tunics were brown, while the most expensive were dyed purple. Some stylish young Romans wore brightly coloured or embroidered tunics with matching shoes. Slaves normally wore cheap tunics, although some wealthy owners liked to dress their slaves in smart tunics made of good-quality material. Tunics allowed ease of movement and

This 3rd century AD Roman mosaic shows the poet Virgil wearing a toga over a tunic

were much better suited to a hot climate than the toga. However, if the wearer felt cold, he could wear more than one tunic. When visiting a friend's house for dinner parties, Roman men often changed out of their togas into a more comfortable, loose gown called a *synthesis*.

Sometimes men might also wear a woollen cloak (*lacerna* or *pallium*). Romans did not normally wear hats, although country folk might wear a broad-brimmed hat (*petasus*) to protect them from the sun. Both men and women wore sandals (*soleae*) or slippers (*crepidae*) indoors. (Slippers known as *socci* were worn by women only.) Heavier shoes called *calcei* were worn outdoors.

Roman women were keen observers of the latest trends. In particular, rich Roman women spent an enormous amount of time and money on the newest hairstyles, the best make-up and the smartest jewellery, partly to enrich the simplicity of their clothing. Roman women wore a tunic and a dress (*stola*, sometimes even made from silk imported from China), with a cloak (*palla*) for protection outdoors.

Getting dressed was a time-consuming business for a wealthy Roman woman. She would direct her maidservants (*ancillae* or *ornatrices*) to arrange her hair in the latest style. A tweaked lock or a badly arranged curl might result in a beating from an irate mistress. If the woman's hair was not suitable for her preferred look, she might dye her hair or wear a wig.

The next task was applying make-up. Roman women used a great deal of make-up. First came white lead, to produce a fashionably pale face. Unfortunately, lead might well eventually poison its wearer or cause unsightly blotches on the face. Red ochre or left-over wine was used as blusher and lipstick, powdered antimony for eyeshadow, mascara for eyelashes and a type of eye-liner to highlight the eyes. Perfume varied in cost and quality from the extremely expensive imports of Egypt and the east to cheaper products made in Italy.

Finally, a woman would select her jewellery. Archaeologists have discovered a vast range of Roman jewellery across the empire: bracelets, rings, necklaces, pendants, earrings, hair clasps, elaborate brooches and pins. Rich women could afford a wide variety of silver and gold ornaments, sometimes inlaid with fine jewels, such as sapphires, pearls or emeralds. However, even poor women possessed jewellery made from carved and polished bone or wood.

Roman boys and girls wore small versions of adult clothes, rather than items specifically designed as childrenswear. However, they also wore a lucky charm (*bulla*) on a string round their necks. Children from wealthy families would have a *bulla* made from gold or bronze, whereas children from poor families would wear a *bulla* made from leather. The *bulla* was worn throughout childhood. Boys dedicated their *bulla* to the household gods when they celebrated their coming-of-age ceremony and girls dedicated theirs on the eve of their wedding. Both rituals showed that childhood had ended and adult life had begun.

7.2 Food and meals

Romans enjoyed a typical Mediterranean diet, rich in vegetables and fish. Meat was expensive and ordinary people seldom ate it. The Romans took food seriously and saw meals as a time to socialise and enjoy each other's company.

Romans did not eat much at breakfast or midday. The early morning meal (*ientaculum*) consisted of a drink of water or wine and some bread, perhaps served with fruit, olives or honey. Lunch (*prandium*) was normally a cold snack, such as bread accompanied by fruit, cheese, olives, vegetables or dried figs. Food left over from the previous dinner might also be eaten. The main meal of the day was dinner (*cena*), which was served in the afternoon. Poor people might eat a wheat porridge or bread, fish, vegetables or fruit washed down with some cheap wine. Wealthier Romans would have a three-course dinner, which was eaten in the dining room (*triclinium*), with diners reclining on couches. Normally, three people reclined on each couch and there were three couches (*lecti*) placed around a circular table (*mensa*). Slaves served the meals from the fourth side. Large banquets might also be held, with two or more sets of couches.

In this 4th century wall painting the diners are reclining on couches while slaves serve food

A three-course dinner was divided into **gustatio** (starters), **primae mensae** (main course) and **secundae mensae** (dessert course). Starters included olives, egg dishes, vegetable and fish snacks, dried fruit and nuts. The main course could include fish, game, poultry, mutton, beef or pork served in a variety of sauces and spices. A particularly popular sauce was a smelly fish sauce called **garum**. Highly prized delicacies included dormice (**glires**), snails, turbot, lampreys, oysters, mullet, boar, stork and peacock. At ostentatious banquets, the food was sometimes elaborately arranged – for example, a bird would be served cooked but covered in its own feathers. The dessert course included fruit (such as apples, plums, grapes, cherries and dates) and sweet cakes. Since sugar had not yet been brought to Europe, honey was used to sweeten food. To accompany the meal the Romans drank wine or water. The finest wine was believed to come from the Falernian region of Italy, although the Romans also drank wine sweetened with honey (**mulsum**).

ROMANS

Food was served cut up into small pieces and diners used their fingers or spoons to eat. Guests were provided with napkins (*mappae*) to clean their hands and they sometimes took left-over food home with them in their napkins. Both guests and host wore garlands of flowers (*coronae*) on their heads.

Entertainment at a dinner party varied. Some hosts invited friends to discuss politics and current affairs. Other hosts provided entertainment such as singers, musicians or acrobats and jugglers. After dinner, it was common for guests to recite poetry or play music. If a drinking party (*commissatio*) followed dinner, the main emphasis was on drinking wine, but slave girls were often brought in to sing to the guests.

7.3 Roman housing: the domus

Roman houses varied in size and layout. Townhouses had a different layout from farmhouses in the country and the dwellings of the poor were much smaller than the houses of the rich. The poorest city dwellers lived in apartment blocks known as *insulae* (detached block of flats), whereas middle-class or rich Romans lived in private townhouses. Townhouses were found throughout the Roman Empire and, although they varied in size according to the wealth of the owner, each townhouse (*domus*) followed a similar basic plan.

A typical *domus* was built round an inner courtyard and was normally one storey high, although some had two storeys. While some of the inner rooms looked out onto the courtyard and garden, the outer walls of a *domus* had few, if any, windows. This

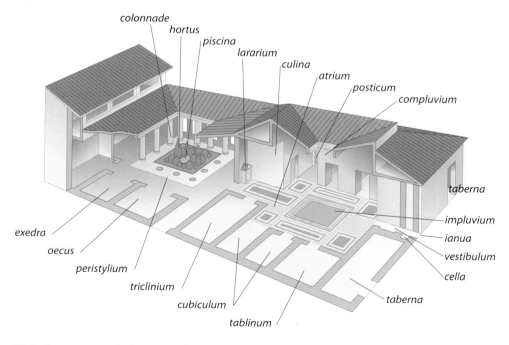

Rich Romans might live in a domus *or town house typically arranged as in this plan*

lack of windows made the domus much more secure and prevented thieves from breaking in.

A *domus* often had two entrances. The back door, known as the **posticum**, was situated near the kitchen and slaves' quarters. The main entrance led off the street and was approached from the porch (**vestibulum**). The doorway (**ianua**) was guarded by a door-keeper who sat in the door-keeper's room (**cella**) just inside the house. The door-keeper was normally a strong slave who was capable of seeing off undesirable visitors. If visitors were admitted to the *domus*, they left the porch and entered the entrance hall (**atrium**).

The *atrium* was a large room which was often used to entertain guests. *Atria* were decorated with fine wall paintings and mosaic floors and they had tall pillars which supported the roof. These pillars were often made of marble, or wood that was painted to look like marble. In the middle of the *atrium* roof was an opening, called the **compluvium**. The *compluvium* provided light and also channelled rainwater from the roof down into a large basin in the centre of the *atrium* called the **impluvium**.

The *atrium* was where the family strongbox (**arca**) was kept and was also the focus of much family religious activity. The **lararium**, or shrine to the family gods (**lares**), was normally found in a corner of the *atrium*. The *lares* were believed to protect the house and its inhabitants. Prayers for the health and safety of the family were said in front of the *lararium* most mornings. Masks (**imagines**) or busts of famous ancestors were kept in an alcove (**ala**) off the *atrium*. Most houses seem to have had two *alae*.

Family bedrooms (**cubicula**; singular = **cubiculum**) led off from the *atrium*, as did the study (**tablinum**) and dining room (**triclinium**). The *tablinum* generally faced out onto the courtyard garden and was often a light, airy room. It was mostly used as a reception room for special friends or important visitors, particularly if the master of the house was transacting business or dealing with politics. The *triclinium* was where formal meals were eaten. Diners did not sit at a dining table, but ate reclining on couches. There were three couches and normally three guests per couch (**lectus**).

The quarters at the back of a Roman *domus* were arranged round the colonnaded courtyard garden (**peristylium**). This was designed to provide both light (in

A domus *had a colonnaded courtyard garden, often laid out in a formal style such as in this reconstruction in Pompeii*

the open part of the garden) and shade (under the colonnade). The colonnade was a passageway with a roof supported by columns. Although the colonnade had evolved to provide shade from the fierce Italian sunshine, the design was utilised throughout the empire, including in Britain. The garden (*hortus*) contained both trees (such as olive, cypress and plane trees) and a variety of ornamental plants. Roses, lilies, poppies and various herbs were all popular. Some houses had an ornamental pool (*piscina*) in the *peristylium* and such pools were often stocked with decorative fish. Two garden rooms known as the *oecus* (outdoor dining room) and *exedra* (outdoor sitting room) could be found to the side of the *peristylium*. The kitchen (*culina*) was near the back door (*posticum*) as were the lavatories (*latrinae*) and slaves' quarters.

Many townhouses had shops (*tabernae*; singular = *taberna*) on either side of the main entrance. These shops were built as part of the *domus*, and were rented out as a useful source of revenue for the owner of the *domus*.

7.4 Flats and country houses

While the *domus* was a comfortable and spacious home, most town dwellers lived in much more cramped conditions in apartment blocks (*insulae*). *Insulae* were four or five storeys tall, although the Emperor Augustus restricted their maximum height to 20 metres. *Insulae* were constructed from wood, brick and concrete, but they were often shoddily built without proper foundations. There was a real danger of the blocks collapsing and killing their occupants. People who lived in *insulae* also faced the danger of fire. Although the Emperor Augustus set up the **vigiles** (a force of 7,000 men whose duty it was to put out fires in Rome), many towns had no proper fire brigade. It was also very difficult to put out burning buildings when water had to be brought from the nearest fountain or aqueduct.

While some expensive and well-maintained *insulae* were built, in general, life in these apartment blocks was cramped, noisy, smelly and sometimes dangerous. Each flat (*cenaculum*) in the *insula* consisted of a few rooms with no running water or proper cooking facilities. Sometimes two or more families might be packed into the small, overcrowded rooms. The ground floor flats were often used for shops. The first floor flats appear to have been the most desirable and the flats in the attic storey the least desirable. Attic flats cost the least to rent, partly because such flats offered no escape in the case of a fire.

Just as in towns, living conditions in the country partly depended on wealth. Poor people lived in small cottages known as *casae*, while wealthier people owned *villae* (villas). Some well-off Romans owned houses in both the town and the country and retreated to their villas during the hot summer months.

There were two types of Roman villa. The **villa rustica** was a farmhouse that was attached to a working farm. As well as rooms in which to live and sleep, many *villae rusticae* had storerooms for farm produce, as well as outbuildings. These included barns and stables, where animals might be kept. Often villas also had a wine press for crushing grapes, a wine cellar to store the finished product and a threshing floor for winnowing grain. The ***villa urbana*** was a country house owned by very wealthy people. It was a luxurious house suitable for those with sophisticated urban tastes and was normally much larger than a townhouse, with a less regular layout of rooms. There was space for colonnaded walks and a

Poor and moderately well-off Romans lived in apartment blocks; the cheapest rooms were found highest up

private bath-house. The *villa urbana* also had fine views over the surrounding countryside and was a place for relaxation, away from the cares of the city. Although the *villa urbana* was generally located on a large country estate, it was not normally a working farmhouse (which would be located separately). Instead, these country houses had fine decoration and furniture and were a source of pride to their rich owners. Some of the most expensive and magnificent country houses were found on the Bay of Naples.

7.5 Interiors and amenities

Decoration and furniture

Houses were often decorated with mosaic floors. Mosaics were made up of hundreds of small cubes of different coloured stone set in mortar. Sometimes coloured glass was used in mosaics to help catch the light. Many mosaics had geometric patterns, but more expensive mosaics might show portraits of the gods, hunting scenes or scenes from mythology. Some mosaics had themes that were particularly appropriate to the use of the room. For example,

This magnificent mosaic of Cupid on a dolphin can be found at the Roman palace of Fishbourne in Sussex

designs of waves, fish and sea creatures were popular in private bath-houses. Black and white mosaics appear to have been less costly than coloured mosaics, but many surviving black and white mosaics are very striking and effective.

Roman houses also had decorated walls. Unlike in modern houses, paintings were painted directly onto the walls. These wall paintings are known as frescoes and were common in the homes of rich Romans. Popular subjects for frescoes were mythology, battle scenes and pictures of still life (for example, paintings of fruit, game birds or wine jugs). Pastoral scenes were also popular, particularly large paintings that gave the impression that the onlooker was actually gazing out directly onto the countryside.

Many well-off Romans decorated their homes with statues. Statues varied in size from small statuettes less than thirty centimetres high to life-size portrayals of the gods or famous ancestors. Some Romans even had statues of themselves and their immediate family in their homes – this was particularly common if the owner of the house was a senator or another important official. Statues were normally made of

73

marble, although very valuable statues were also made of bronze or – on rare occasions – gold.

Roman houses had much less furniture than modern houses. When relaxing, Romans reclined, rather than sat, and they used couches rather than chairs. They did not lie down on the couches, but propped up their bodies by leaning on one elbow. Rich Romans reclined even at dinner and dining rooms had three couches, rather than a formal dining table with chairs. Normally, three people shared a couch (*lectus*) and food was placed on a low table next to the couch. Although a few chairs (**sellae**) were used in reception rooms, these were kept for important visitors. Young children and slaves sat on stools (**scamna**). Other furniture included tables and storage cupboards.

Bedroom furniture was equally limited. Beds were made from a wooden frame with slings of rope or rawhide strips. A mattress, cushions and bedclothes were placed on top. Poor people might use a mattress made of straw or have no mattress at all. Rich people tended to have more comfortable mattresses stuffed with wool. Pillows were also stuffed with wool or down.

The Pont du Gard, a Roman aqueduct near Nîmes, South of France

Ordinary furniture was made out of wood. Expensive furniture was made out of much finer materials: marble, ivory, bronze and gold were all used. Sometimes expensive inlays of tortoiseshell, silver or costly woods (such as ebony) might be used to create a fine pattern on the furniture.

Amenities

Roman houses lacked many of the amenities that we take for granted. There was no electricity or gas and, for most people, the closest thing to running water was a fountain at the end of a street. (The rich might pay for a pipe to bring water from the nearest aqueduct to a storage tank in their house.) Only very rich Romans had private bath-houses with hot and cold baths; everyone else used public bath-houses.

However, both the very rich and the moderately wealthy inhabitants of a *domus* had access to their own lavatory (*latrina*), whereas flat dwellers did not. Instead, they used public facilities or a chamber pot, which was emptied into the drains.

Lighting was provided by oil lamps, which burned olive oil. The light was not as clear as that provided nowadays by electric bulbs and the cheaper the olive oil, the smokier the light that was produced. Ordinary lamps were made out of terracotta (a kind of clay), although more elegant, expensive lamps were also made from bronze or copper. An elaborate lamp called a **candelabrum** burned several separate oil lamps at once.

Although each *domus* had a kitchen (*culina*), people who lived in flats did not have proper cooking facilities. They either used a small, portable brazier or ate hot food only when they bought it from taverns (*tabernae*) or shops that sold hot snacks (**popinae**). Stalls that specialised in hot or cold drinks (**thermopolia**) might also sell a selection of nibbles such as sausages, cheese, dates, figs and cake.

Heating varied according to the type of house. People living in flats kept warm by using portable braziers. However, there was a great risk of these falling over and setting the *insula* on fire. Although braziers might be used to heat an individual room in a *domus*, most houses were equipped with a hypocaust (see diagram page 61), where hot air circulated under the floor. The hypocaust was an effective heating system, although it did require slaves to crawl under the floors to clean the flues and to stoke the furnace.

In towns, gardens were restricted to the *domus*. There were a few public gardens, but ordinary Romans lived in a world of buildings and streets, rather than green spaces.

Exercise 7.1

1. (a) Give a detailed description of the clothes that men wore in Roman times.
   (b) How comfortable do you think Roman clothes would have been? Explain your answer.
2. (a) Describe the various clothes worn by Roman women and the jewellery and make-up they used.
   (b) Name one similarity and one difference between Roman and modern fashion.
3. (a) Write a description of the clothes and charms worn by Roman children and slaves.
   (b) Why do you think that Roman parents wanted their children to wear a *bulla*?

Extension work

Hold a Roman fashion show! Divide your class into four groups and assign each group to focus on men's, women's, boys' or girls' clothes. Each group will need to carry out further research into what Roman clothes looked like. You may choose to present the fashion show either with real clothing or with large posters displaying your design. Try to use different colours and fabrics and make sure you include Latin names.

Exercise 7.2

1. (a) Describe the different meals that the Romans ate and give examples of food that might have been eaten at each meal.
    (b) Name one similarity and one difference between Roman and modern eating habits.
2. (a) Imagine you are attending a dinner party given by a wealthy Roman. Describe the evening.
    (b) What would you most have enjoyed about attending such a dinner and why do you think this?
3. (a) Describe the differences between how rich and poor people dined and outline what sort of entertainment was on offer at a Roman dinner party.
    (b) Why did the Romans think that meals were important occasions and not just an opportunity to eat?

Extension work

One of the first cookery books was written by a Roman called Apicius. Carry out further research and then design your own dinner menu based on his recipes. Explain which recipe you would most enjoy. You might even try cooking some of them at home.

Exercise 7.3

1. (a) Describe the main rooms of a Roman *domus*.
    (b) Why do you think the Romans regarded the *atrium* as the most important room of the house?
2. (a) Describe the rooms in the slave quarters and the rooms that surrounded the garden of a Roman *domus*.
    (b) Which do you think would have been the most attractive room in a Roman *domus* and why do you think this?
3. (a) Draw a diagram of a typical Roman *domus* and label as many features as you can in both English and Latin.
    (b) Explain two differences between the uses of a Roman *atrium* and the main room of a modern house.

Extension work

Imagine that you are a wealthy Roman. Design your ideal *domus*.

Exercise 7.4

1. (a) Explain why life was difficult for poor people who lived in flats.
   (b) What do you think would have been the worst aspect of living in a Roman apartment block? Explain your answer.
2. (a) Describe the different types of housing that were available in the countryside.
   (b) Name one similarity and one difference between a *villa rustica* and a modern farmhouse.
3. (a) Many rich Romans had houses both in the country and in Rome itself. Outline the main advantages of each type of house.
   (b) Which sort of house would you most enjoy living in and why do you think this?

Extension work

Carry out further research into the lives of poor people in Rome. Did any political leaders offer to make their lives better and did they succeed in this aim? Write an essay setting out your findings.

Exercise 7.5

1. (a) What sort of decoration was available in Roman houses?
   (b) Which form of Roman decoration would you most like to have in your home and why do you think this?
2. (a) Describe the various items of furniture used by Romans in their houses, including the materials that were used in their manufacture.
   (b) Name one similarity and one difference between Roman furniture and furniture found in modern homes.
3. (a) Describe the amenities that the Romans had available in their homes.
   (b) Name one modern amenity that you would most miss if you lived in Roman times and explain why you think this.

Extension work

Think about the sort of images that would be particularly appropriate for the frescoes of the *triclinium* of a Roman house and then produce your own designs.

> Remember that the Roman baths are part of the Domestic Life syllabus for Common Entrance. Read the information on pages 60–63 and answer Exercise 6.4.

CHAPTER 8 LIFE, DEATH AND SLAVERY

8.1 Adulthood

Coming of age

Although many Roman boys assumed adult roles (such as working) when they were quite young, boys officially entered adulthood when they held their coming-of-age ceremony. This was normally celebrated around the age of fourteen, although there was no fixed age. The ceremony was often held at the festival of Liberalia (17th March), rather than on the boy's actual birthday.

A coming-of-age ceremony began with a short service during which the boy approached the *lararium* (shrine to the household gods). Here he dedicated his *toga praetexta* and his *bulla* (lucky charm), which he had worn since infancy, to the household gods. He then put on the *toga virilis* (plain white toga), which was worn by adult male citizens.

After the dedications to the household gods were over, the boy's family and friends led him to the records building (**tabularium**) in the forum. Here his name was entered in the records (**tabulae**) of citizens. The young man was now eligible to vote in elections and could prove that he was a citizen. Amid great rejoicing, the family returned home to celebrate with a party. Girls were believed to reach adulthood when they married and so did not celebrate coming of age as boys did.

Marriage

Roman marriages could occur when both bride and groom were very young. Roman boys could marry from the age of fourteen and girls from the age of twelve. Although most men married in their late teens or twenties, girls often married when they were fourteen. Most Roman marriages were arranged by the parents of the bride, who would choose a suitable man to marry their daughter. Wealthy or important political families used their children to strengthen business interests or to cement political friendships. Some children were betrothed to each other when they were still in their cradles. Although such marriages were not love matches, many couples did grow to like each other.

The first step to marriage was the announcement of the engagement. An engagement party (**sponsalia**) was held where the bride and groom exchanged presents (such as rings). This was also the time when the marriage contract was signed and witnessed. The marriage contract related to the dowry (**dos**), the gift that a bride's father (or closest relative) gave to the bridegroom. The dowry was normally a sum of money, an amount of land or the ownership of buildings. Poor fathers might provide a dowry of farm livestock.

Romans could become legally married either by living together as man and wife for a year or by stating in front of witnesses that they were married. However, many Romans chose to go through a formal wedding ceremony. On the night before the wedding, the bride dedicated her childhood toys and her *bulla* to the family gods in the *lararium*. The wedding was held at the house of the bride's parents, which was decorated with flowers and leaves tied up with ribbons. The masks (*imagines*) of famous ancestors were also put on display.

On the wedding day, the bride dressed carefully in a long white dress (***tunica recta***), over which she wore a saffron-yellow cloak (***palla***). Her hair was parted, according to traditional custom, with an iron spear and arranged into six plaits. Over her head she wore a garland of flowers (***corona***) and a bright orange veil (***flammeum***) and shoes. A married woman (***pronuba***) acted as matron of honour and accompanied the bride to where the guests were waiting. Here the actual wedding ceremony (***nuptiae***) began with a sacrifice to the gods. The priest (***augur***) checked the sacrifice for omens (***auspices***) that the day was favourable for marrying. Next, the marriage contract was signed and the matron of honour joined the right hands of the bride and groom together. This declaration and joining of hands (***dextrarum iunctio***) constituted the formal marriage. Everyone prayed for the couple to have a happy life together and then a second sacrifice was made to the gods.

After the wedding ceremony there was a wedding feast (***cena nuptialis***). At the end of the feast, the bride pretended not to want to leave her parents and the groom snatched her from her mother's arms. The couple then set off to the groom's house, accompanied by their guests, torch-bearers and flute players (***tibicines***). Wedding

Roman weddings often included an elaborate feast,
such as is shown in this 19th century painting

songs were sung and nuts thrown to onlookers. The bride carried a distaff and spindle which showed that, now she was married, her tasks would include spinning and making cloth for her new family. When the procession reached the bridegroom's home, he asked her the traditional question: 'Who are you?' She replied '*ubi tu Gaius, ego Gaia*' ('Where you are Gaius, I am Gaia'). He carried her over the threshold of the house and led her to the marriage couch (*lectus genialis*). The bridegroom next gave the bride fire and water, demonstrating that she was now considered the mistress of the house. The wedding guests then departed, leaving the bride and groom together.

Not all Roman marriages were successful. Divorce was easy to arrange and many Roman marriages ended in divorce, particularly in rich families where shifting political allegiances could see a man leave his wife in order to marry another woman who was more closely linked to his new political allies. However, any dowry had to be returned to his ex-wife, who was free to remarry if she wanted. The need to return a woman's dowry protected her from being turned out penniless. Moreover, women had the right to divorce unsatisfactory husbands, although women were expected to return to their own family after divorce, rather than living on their own or with friends.

8.2 Death and burial

Romans believed that it was very important to bury the dead according to the correct rites. They believed that, if this were not done, the soul of the dead person would never be able to rest. The most important aspects of the ceremony were to scatter three handfuls of dust over the corpse and to put a small coin in the mouth of the dead person. Romans believed that dead souls used this coin to pay Charon, the ferryman of the dead, to row them across the River Styx to the Underworld.

Although poor people were normally buried at night in a common grave without much ceremony, the funeral of a member of a rich or important family was very elaborate. The body was washed with warm water, anointed with sweet-smelling oils and dressed in its best clothes. The body lay in state on a funeral couch (*lectus funebris*) in the *atrium* of the family's townhouse. Lamps (*lucernae*) and candles (*candelae*) were placed round the body and the mourners filed past the corpse, paying their last respects. Cypress or pine branches were placed outside the house to show that someone had died.

On the day of the funeral, the funeral procession (*pompa funebris*) gathered at the house of the dead person, before setting off through the city to the forum. Flute players (*tibicines*) and trumpet players (*cornicines*) marched at the head of the procession, followed by men carrying the litter with the dead body. Torch-bearers walked behind the litter, accompanied by professional mourners (*praeficae*) and singers of sad songs. The professional mourners often beat their breasts, wailing loudly and tearing at their clothing and hair. Slaves who had been freed by the dead man also walked in the procession, increasing the numbers – an important method of indicating the importance of the dead person. Next came relatives of the dead. Male members of the family carried masks (*imagines*) of ancestors and any crowns (*coronae*) or military honours that the dead man had been awarded. If the dead man had been a magistrate, then public attendants (*lictores*) might be present, carrying the *fasces*, which were the symbol of office of a magistrate. Finally, friends of the dead made up the end of the procession, sometimes followed by curious onlookers.

When the procession reached the forum, it halted while the dead man's son or nearest relative gave a speech (*laudatio*) praising the dead man's deeds and the acts of his ancestors. Occasionally, powerful families would give a *laudatio* for a dead woman, praising her modesty and referring to the importance of her family. The procession then moved on to the family tomb, which was outside the city walls. Here, the body was buried along with some of the dead person's possessions. It was thought that the dead would need various things in the afterlife (for example, toys might be buried with a child and jewellery with a woman).

The funeral procession is shown in this 1st century BC relief

Sometimes bodies were cremated on a funeral pyre (*pyra*). A family member set fire to the pyre and onlookers threw perfume, flowers and spices onto the fire. After the fire had burned down, wine was poured over the ashes to cool them. The ashes were then placed in an urn (*urna*) and put into the family tomb. The ashes of poorer citizens were buried in an underground chamber called a *columbarium*, where hundreds of urns were gathered together to save space.

The grieving family then observed nine days of official mourning. When this ended, the family brought an offering of food to the tomb and presented it to the spirits (*manes*) of the dead man. Relatives often brought food, milk and wine to the tomb on the anniversary of a man's death or on important family occasions.

8.3 Slavery

Sources and duties

Slavery is one of the least attractive aspects of the Roman world. Today, most people consider the idea of one person owning another abhorrent. However, in Roman times, the practice was very common although, unlike most Greek slaves, Roman slaves did have some chance of gaining their freedom. Roman society was also sufficiently open to allow freedmen and their children to gain positions of great responsibility within the Roman state.

There were many ways in which people might fall into slavery. Enormous numbers of men, women and children were captured in wars, either by the victorious Romans or by other nations. A few might be ransomed by relatives, but the vast majority were enslaved. People might also be kidnapped or captured by pirates and then sold into slavery. Children were another source of slaves. Unwanted children were abandoned (or 'exposed') by their parents (normally at birth). They were sometimes saved from death by exposure, only to be brought up as slaves. Some abandoned children remained within the family which had raised them, but others were sold when they were old enough to fetch a good price. Children who were born to slave parents automatically took the status of slaves. However, such children (known as *vernae*) were normally part of a settled household and were usually better treated than slaves who were bought from a slave market.

Most people bought their slaves from slave dealers (*mangones* or *venalicii*). Slaves were put on display on a platform so that potential purchasers could inspect them. Each slave had a scroll (*titulus*) round their neck, which described their skills. The more skilled the slave, the more the slave would cost. For example, a doctor, a singer or a man who could keep accounts would fetch much more than a farm labourer. In general, more expensive slaves were better treated since they would cost more to replace.

Certain regions of the world were believed to produce slaves who were particularly good at certain tasks. For example, educated Greek slaves were considered highly desirable as tutors for Roman children.

The duties of slaves varied considerably according to whether they were used for domestic work, agricultural labour or industry. Slaves were used for an enormous variety of tasks within Roman society – some worked long hours in dangerous conditions in the mines while others were based in the emperor's palace, keeping the imperial accounts and exerting considerable influence over Roman citizens. Between these two extremes, slaves could be found working as hairdressers, porters, gardeners, cleaners, teachers, farm bailiffs, household overseers, secretaries, cooks, acrobats, musicians, singers, dancers and actors.

Poor Romans might well have one or two slaves to help with general domestic tasks and perhaps to assist with running their business (for example, as a shoe maker or a potter). Rich Romans owned many slaves and, as well as all-purpose workers, often had many specialist slaves. Such slaves would include a cook (***coquus***), a hairdresser or barber (***tonsor***), a tutor (***praeceptor domesticus***) to teach the children and a slave who took the sons of the house to and from school (***paedagogus***). Other specialist slaves included a secretary (***amanuensis***), librarian (***bibliothecarius***), accountant (***calculator***) and physician (***medicus***). Rich Roman women would possess many personal maidservants (***ancillae***) who would help them to dress, to arrange their hair and to apply their make-up. Rich Romans also had female slaves to clean, cook and weave clothes for the household.

Some rich Romans bought slaves and set them up in their own business. The owner took the largest share of the profits, but the slave had some liberty and the chance to make enough money to eventually buy his freedom. According to their individual skills, slaves might be set up either in specialist trades (such as goldsmiths or metalworkers) or ordinary trades (such as bakers).

Some slaves were owned by the state and employed in public administration. These state slaves (***servi publici***) could rise to positions of considerable importance and

*Slaves were a vital part of Roman society; this mosaic
shows slaves serving at a banquet*

were a vital part of the Roman Empire as they looked after most of the records and accounts. Other state slaves maintained public buildings such as aqueducts and bridges.

The worst type of work for a slave was heavy labour on farms or in mines. Many Roman farms were large estates, which were run almost entirely by slave labour. These farms (**latifundia**) usually had a farm manager or bailiff (**vilicus**) who was also a slave. A *vilicus* had normally begun work as an ordinary labourer and would be very keen not to lose his promotion. He would work the other slaves hard to try to make as much money for his master as possible, knowing that he had a chance of freedom if his master were pleased with him. As well as labouring in the fields, slaves also worked as shepherds, cowherds and goatherds.

Work in the mines was regarded as the worst role of all and slaves were threatened with being sold to the mines if they were disobedient. Mining slaves were given little food and they often worked, lived and slept underground. Miners worked long hours carrying out hard physical labour, with the risk of dying in a rock fall or if the air became bad. Mining slaves were treated like animals and were beaten if they did not work hard enough. Slaves in the mines had almost no chance of gaining their freedom and many died after only a few years. Some slaves worked in quarries, rather than mines, but, apart from the fact that the work was in the open, there was no difference in the way they were treated.

Conditions and treatment

In general, slaves who worked in their owner's home were better treated than those who worked on large farms or in the mines. Domestic slaves had more chance of being regarded as one of the family, whereas slaves who worked in large gangs had little individual identity and were seen as pieces of equipment. Mine slaves normally left the mines only when they died, while farm slaves had no security and could be sold at any moment. One Roman author (Cato the Elder) even advised selling off old or weak slaves for whatever price you could get when they were no longer capable of hard work.

Slaves were utterly in their owner's power and could be very badly treated – beatings were common and slaves could be killed by their masters. Although murdering a slave was illegal, an owner was unlikely to be prosecuted, particularly if he could provide a reason for killing the slave. However, most slave owners did not want to lose the cost of their investment and therefore ensured their slaves were reasonably well treated. Some slave owners treated their slaves very well and regarded them as friends. Despite this, slaves had little security – the death of their master or mistress might see a slave handed over to a new, cruel owner.

Slaves were in no position to retaliate if they were badly treated. If they struck their owner they could be flogged or put to death. If a slave killed his master, by law the entire household of slaves was put to death. Slaves who rebelled were crucified, as happened to 6,000 slaves who joined a rebel slave army led by Spartacus in 73–71 BC.

Slaves who ran away were also cruelly punished. When caught, runaways were harshly flogged and had the letter 'F' (for ***fugitivus***) branded on their foreheads so that everyone could see that they were untrustworthy. A domestic slave who ran away would often be sent to work in the mines, or as part of a labour gang on a farm. The risks of terrible punishment deterred many slaves from running away. Many of those who did flee ended up joining bands of robbers as they dared not risk recapture.

Roman law reflected the low status of slaves. Slaves were seen as possessions, not as human beings with feelings, thoughts and hopes. Evidence from a slave was only legally acceptable if it had been extracted under torture and slaves had no legal right to own property or to marry. However, unofficial relationships were tolerated between male and female slaves and most owners allowed any children born of such relationships to stay within the household. Normally, slaves were allowed to have some personal belongings. Slaves were also able to keep some pocket money (***peculium***), which they earned from tips, bribes or carrying out extra work when they were off duty. Slaves who had been set up in business by their owners were also given a percentage of what they earned.

Apart from the toga, slaves wore the same sort of clothes as ordinary Roman citizens and there were no restrictions on them visiting various public attractions such as the theatre. Slaves were a common sight on the streets of Roman cities and, in Rome, made up a large percentage of the population. It has been calculated that, in Italy in the first century AD, three out of every eight men were slaves.

Freedom

Slaves could gain their freedom in a number of ways. Manumission (***manumissio***) might be granted to a slave as a reward for performing some very important act for his owner, such as saving his life. Long and loyal service might also see a slave manumitted. Sometimes slaves were able to buy their freedom with their savings, although it might take them years to save enough money. Many slaves were freed in their owner's will. However, Roman law restricted such manumissions in wills to slaves over the age of thirty and no more than one hundred slaves could be freed from a large household. This law had come into practice after wealthy slave owners had taken to showing off their vast wealth by freeing hundreds of their slaves in their wills.

When a slave was freed, there was a short manumission ceremony. Roman citizens had three names and freedmen added the family names of their master to their own name. Thus many freed slaves had a mixture of a foreign last name and two traditional Roman names. At the same time as acquiring a new name, the slave was given a cap of freedom (***pilleus***). This indicated that the slave no longer belonged to someone, but was a freedman (***libertus***) or freedwoman (***liberta***). From now on the slave's former master (***dominus***) became his patron (***patronus***). In turn, the ex-slave became a client (***cliens***) of the former master. Although the patron no longer had the power of life or death over his former slave, a freedman was expected to work for him for a number of days each year, or to make a cash payment instead. A freedman had to show great respect to his patron and to help him whenever possible. Such help included accompanying his patron to the forum. This was particularly important if the patron was involved in politics – politicians liked to be seen surrounded by a crowd of eager supporters.

Most days, the freedman visited his patron's house early in the morning to see if his patron required his company. In response to this formal visit (**salutatio**), the patron might give his client a small sum of money (**sportula** – normally set at 6¼ *sestertii*) or invite him to dinner. Patrons were also expected to help their *clientes* if they were in trouble and to give them advice.

Although a freedman became a citizen, he did not have the same rights as a full Roman citizen: he could not stand in public elections nor was he allowed to serve as an important army officer. However, any children born to freed parents after the manumission ceremony were born full Roman citizens. Many former slaves prospered after they were manumitted and some freedmen became immensely wealthy. The Roman author Petronius wrote a novel called *The Satyricon*, which described the life of an extremely rich former slave called Trimalchio. Trimalchio is shown enjoying an extravagant lifestyle, living in a vast mansion surrounded by hundreds of slaves and spending large sums of money on entertaining. However, some former slaves found life very difficult after they were set free. They had no particular training for a trade and the jobs that they were used to doing (such as cleaning or cooking) were normally carried out by slaves, rather than by hired servants. Although they may have desperately wanted to be free, sometimes they became much worse off. At least, as a slave, they would have been fed – some freedmen were so poor that they ate less food than they had as a slave.

Exercise 8.1

1. (a) Imagine you are a Roman teenager. Describe your best friend's coming-of-age ceremony.
   (b) Can you think of any modern rituals (either religious or secular) that are similar to Roman coming-of-age ceremonies?

2. (a) Explain the events of a Roman engagement party and what important families might be looking to gain from a marriage.
   (b) Do you think there was any protection for women who got divorced? Explain your answer.

3. (a) Give a detailed description of a Roman wedding ceremony and feast.
   (b) Name two differences between Roman weddings and modern weddings.

Extension work

Ancient vase paintings and frescoes often had detailed pictures of important ceremonies. Investigate various examples and then design a vase or fresco showing either a Roman coming-of-age ceremony or a Roman marriage ceremony.

Exercise 8.2

1. (a) Give a detailed account of the burial of a rich Roman.
   (b) Why do you think that there was so much ceremony associated with such burials?

2. (a) Describe how poor people were buried and why the Romans thought that it was important to bury the dead properly.
   What might be placed in graves and what sort of offerings were brought to graves after burials?
   (b) Name one similarity and one difference between Roman and modern customs surrounding death and burial.

3. (a) Imagine you have watched the burial of an important Roman politician. Write an atmospheric description of what happened to send to your best friend in Greece.
   (b) Why do you think professional mourners were common at Roman funerals? Explain your answer.

Extension work

Research one important Roman politician and then write the speech to be delivered at his funeral. Deliver your speech to your class.

Exercise 8.3

1. (a) Describe how people might become slaves; explain how they were sold and why some slaves cost more than others.
   (b) What do you think would be the worst type of job that a slave might have to do and why do you think this?

2. (a) Imagine that you are a rich Roman slave owner. Describe what kinds of slaves you have (both in Rome and on your country estate) and how you treat them.
   (b) Why do you think that the Romans accepted large numbers of slaves as part of their society?

3. (a) Describe the ways in which Roman slaves might gain their freedom and what practical steps were taken to mark their manumission.
   (b) Some slaves and freedmen ended up in positions of great influence within the Roman Empire. If you had been a Roman citizen, would you have trusted such people? Explain your answer.

Extension work

Write the biography of a slave, remembering to explain how he or she became a slave and what happened if he or she was freed.

CHAPTER 9 THE ARMY AND ROMAN BRITAIN

9.1 The legion and the Roman army

The Roman army was the greatest instrument of Roman power and, like many aspects of Roman government, was clearly structured. The main organisational unit was the legion and, by the time of the Emperor Augustus (27 BC–AD 14), there were twenty-eight legions, each with their own officers and soldiers. Legions were numbered and many had a name as well. Sometimes this name reflected their bravery (for example, the XX Legion was called the *Valeria Victrix* – 'the victorious Valerian legion'). Legionaries were professional soldiers who were attracted by the excitement of serving in the army or by the pay (especially the gratuity which they received when they retired). Legionaries had to be a citizen or the son of a soldier and they served for twenty-five years, five of which were as a veteran (*veteranus*).

The full strength of each legion was around 5,300 men, although numbers varied, particularly in wartime. The legion was divided up into ten cohorts (*cohortes*) of approximately 480 men. The first cohort was the largest and most important, consisting of 800 men divided into five maniples (*manipuli*) or double-centuries of 160 men. The first cohort was larger than the others because it contained specialists as well as ordinary soldiers. These specialists included engineers (*fabri* or *architecti*), secretaries (*librarii*), doctors (*medici*), vets and priests. Other cohorts

Modern re-enactment groups, such as the Ermine Street Guard,
provide an idea of what Roman soldiers looked like in action

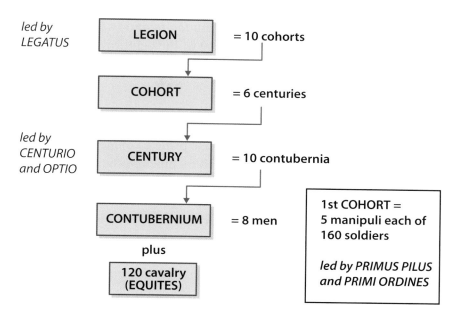

This diagram of a Roman legion shows the clear command structure to each sub-section

were subdivided into six centuries (***centuriae***), with eighty men in each. (Originally, there had been one hundred men in each, hence the name century). Individual centuries were divided into ten sections (***contubernia***) of eight men, who would sleep in the same barrack room or tent.

Each century was commanded by a centurion (***centurio***) and his second-in-command, the ***optio***. Centurions were tough, experienced soldiers who provided vital leadership in battle. The *optio* had a similar role to a non-commissioned officer (NCO) in the British army and was normally a competent fighter with battle experience. Each legion had fifty-nine centurions (since the first century had five – not six – centurions). The most important centurion (***primus pilus*** – 'first spear') led the first century of the first cohort. The camp prefect (***praefectus castrorum***), who organised supplies, equipment and transport, had normally been a *primus pilus*. Other senior centurions also served in the first cohort and were known as ***primi ordines***. Centurions were easily recognisable because they carried a vine staff (***vitis***), which they could use to strike a legionary who had annoyed them. Moreover, their armour was more impressive than that of ordinary soldiers.

In wars, several legions were combined into an army (***exercitus***) and their overall commander (***imperator***) was normally an important figure, such as a consul or ex-consul. The legionary commander (***legatus***) was appointed by the senate or emperor and might not have much military experience. Such commanders usually served for three or four years, before returning to Rome. The *legatus* (who was often a senator) had six tribunes (***tribuni militum***), or staff officers, to help him. The tribunes were often ambitious young men who were gaining experience in the army before running

ROMANS

for political office in Rome. (The Senior Tribune – *tribunus laticlavius* – was particularly likely to be a career politician). Both *legati* and *tribuni* were, therefore, heavily dependent on the advice and experience of the centurions, who were long-serving, professional soldiers, rather than political appointees.

Eagles and auxiliaries

Each legion had a special standard, which was topped by a gold or silver eagle (*aquila*). These eagles were a source of immense pride to the legion (as colours are to a modern regiment) and were carefully guarded by an eagle-bearer (*aquilifer*). It was regarded as disgraceful to lose the eagle of a legion in battle and legions that did might be disbanded and their troops sent to other legions. Each century had its own standard (*signum*) and standard-bearer (*signifer*). Military standards aided recognition and helped a commander to see exactly where each part of the legion was on the battlefield. Each legion also had a *tesserarius*, who was responsible for the passwords. If he served well, he could gain promotion to *signifer*. Trumpeters (*cornicines*) had an important role as signallers, for example, sounding the advance into battle.

As well as the legionary soldiers, each legion had auxiliary forces (*auxilia*) attached to it. Soldiers in the auxiliary units were not citizens, but came from various regions that were under Roman control. If they served for twenty-five years, auxiliaries were granted citizenship when they retired. To avoid the danger of auxiliary troops refusing to fight against their own people, auxiliary units normally served far away from where they were recruited. For example, two *cohortes Tungrorum* (Tungrians) were raised in Belgium, but served in Britain. However, over time, troops began to be recruited locally. Some auxiliaries fought as heavy infantrymen, but others acted as archers (*sagittarii*) or slingers (*funditores*) or served in the cavalry (*equites*). Cavalry fought in battle, but were also used in reconnaissance missions and as despatch riders. Cavalrymen were armed with a long sword (*spatha*) and a thrusting spear (*hasta*), as well as a small, round shield (*clipeus*).

Auxiliary forces were under the command of Roman officers (*praefecti*) aided by decurions (*decuriones*). Decurions were native officers who commanded groups (*turmae*) of thirty horsemen. Cavalry units were organised into wings (*alae*) of 500 or 1,000 men (although the so-called 1,000-man units often contained only around 800 men). Some auxiliaries served in a mixed unit (*cohors equitata*) of light infantry and cavalry.

The Roman army was the main focus of Roman power, but the Romans also used naval forces. Warships (*naves longae*) were used in battle and transport vessels (*naves onerariae*) were vital for moving troops and supplies overseas (such as during the invasion of Britain).

9.2 Equipment

Offensive and defensive equipment

Roman soldiers were often victorious in war. They were highly trained and the command structure of the army meant that it was easy to organise soldiers into effective groups. However, another reason why the Roman soldier was so effective in battle was that he was significantly better equipped than many of his enemies. In particular, the sharp-bladed sword (**gladius**) issued to each legionary was one of the most effective weapons of its time. It was well balanced, lethally sharp and could easily cut through a man. Soldiers also carried two **pila** (singular = **pilum**), which

were two-metre long throwing-spears with an iron head. The spear-head was designed to bend when it hit an obstacle, which meant that the enemy could not throw the spears back at the Romans. Moreover, if a spear struck the shield of an enemy, it was often impossible to remove the spear; thus the enemy had to throw away his now-useless shield. Roman auxiliary troops often used bows and arrows (**sagittae**) or sling-shots. Slingers used small iron balls (**glandes**) or stones (**lapides missiles**), which could be hurled with such force that they broke a man's arm. Spears and arrows

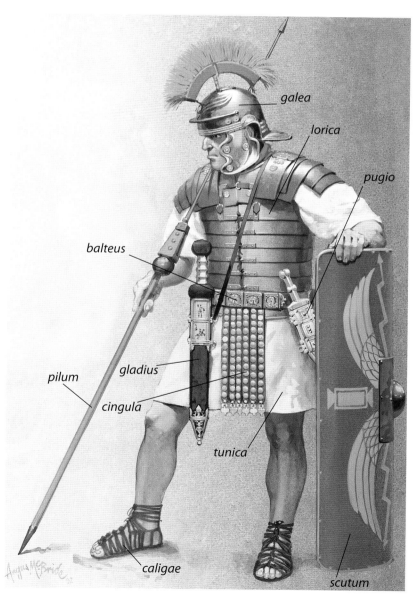

galea
lorica
pugio
balteus
pilum
gladius
cingula
tunica
caligae
scutum

were used at long range, swords were used at close range and each legionary was also equipped with a sharp dagger (***pugio***) for deadly hand-to-hand combat.

A Roman soldier also had good defensive equipment. His head was covered with a bronze or iron helmet (***galea***) and the back of the helmet stuck out to provide protection for the neck. Soldiers protected their bodies with armour (***lorica***), which was worn on top of a woollen tunic (***tunica***). Armour was normally made of a series of overlapping metal strips (***lorica segmentata***), although some soldiers wore a form of chain mail (***lorica hamata***). Both chain mail and the *lorica segmentata* allowed the soldiers to move much more easily than they could in one-piece breastplates. (Officers often wore a breastplate, but theirs were normally custom made to fit their bodies.) A leather belt (***balteus***), which held the legionary's *gladius*, was worn over the *lorica*. Metal-studded leather strips called ***cingula*** hung down from the waist, and soldiers also wore hobnailed boots called ***caligae*** to protect the feet.

One of the most essential pieces of equipment was the shield (***scutum***). This was made of wood covered with leather and was rectangular in shape, curving backwards at the sides. The rims were strengthened with metal and there was a heavy metal boss in the centre of the shield. On the inner side there was a handle with which to hold the shield. Soldiers under attack could link the shields together to provide greater protection and Roman soldiers perfected a technique called the tortoise (***testudo***). This involved the soldiers forming a square or rectangular shape. The front row of soldiers held their shields in front of them and the side columns protected the flanks. However, those in the middle of the square held their shields over their heads, thus ensuring that the entire square was protected by shields. Although only highly disciplined troops could maintain such a position, the *testudo* was difficult to attack and was a very effective defensive position.

Other kit and machines

Soldiers had a woollen cloak, which also served as a blanket at night (officers had a scarlet cloak called a ***paludamentum***). In cold weather, soldiers might wear trousers (***bracae*** or ***braccae***). Although Romans living in Rome sneered at people who wore *bracae*, trousers were more suitable for cold climates, such as Britain. Letters home written by Roman troops in Britain include requests for socks to keep their feet warm!

Roman legionaries carried food and essential kit with them on the march. Each soldier was expected to carry three days' rations, cooking utensils, tools for building a new camp (such as a spade) and wooden stakes to make the camp fence (***vallum***). Mules and pack animals (***iumenta***) were often used to carry heavy items of kit (such as tents) and further food supplies.

As well as manpower, armies used machines, particularly varieties of the torsion-powered ***tormentum***. The *tormentum* gained its power from a rope, which was twisted round and round before being released. The ***onager*** (named after a wild donkey) shot large stones (up to thirty kilograms) at the enemy, sometimes from

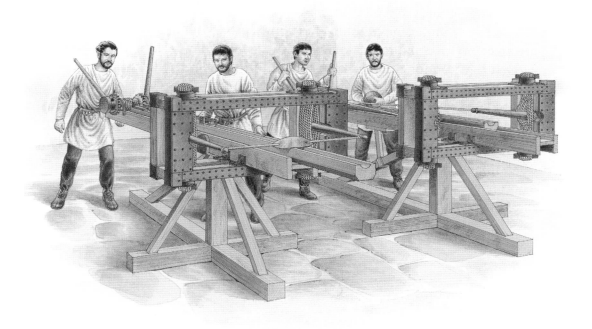

The ballista, *which worked on a torsion principle, was an important weapon during sieges*

800 metres away. The ***ballista*** and ***catapulta*** were less powerful. The *ballista* fired smaller stones, while the *catapulta* shot iron bolts and arrows against men. The *catapulta* also fired burning darts to set wooden defences or buildings on fire. The Romans used siege towers (***turres***) to protect troops approaching well-defended city walls. Walls and ramparts were breached with rams (***arietes***) and walls might also be scaled using scaling ladders (***scalae***).

9.3 Camp

Marching camps and permanent camps

Whenever Roman soldiers were on campaign, they either spent the night in existing army camps or they built temporary camps at the end of each day's march. Soldiers could cover ten to twenty miles (fifteen to thirty kilometres) a day and camps were placed at suitable distances apart. Each camp (***castra***) was rectangular in shape and covered more than half a square mile (a square kilometre). If a legion had to build a temporary camp, the first action was to mark the outline of the camp on the surface of the soil (which was cleared and levelled if necessary). The next essential was to dig a deep ditch (***fossa***) round the four sides of the camp. The *fossa* provided protection from attack, particularly cavalry attacks. The earth from the *fossa* was used to build a rampart (***agger***) and on top of that a wooden palisade (***vallum***) about a metre and a half high would be built from stakes of wood (***valli***). Every soldier carried entrenching tools to dig the ditches and two or three wooden stakes for the *vallum*. When they broke camp, soldiers took the stakes with them to build the next camp. Each camp was built to the same pattern, enabling new camps to be easily built without the need for complicated orders. Moreover, each soldier knew exactly where to find the various buildings within the camp.

Permanent camps (***castra stativa***) had stronger defences than a marching camp and had a wider range of buildings – such as granaries (***horrea***) or a hospital (***valetudinarium***). Each camp required a good supply of water and engineers would assess the suitability of a possible site before agreeing to build the camp. Permanent camps normally had stone or turf ramparts, with towers next to the exits and at the corners of the walls. Many permanent camps had wooden or stone buildings, which were much more comfortable than tents.

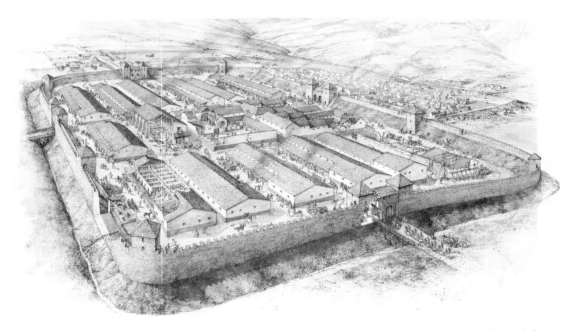

This modern drawing of a Roman permanent camp clearly shows its stone walls and the principia *where the four main roads meet. The* vicus *is outside the camp walls*

There were four exits to a Roman camp (large camps had six), enabling soldiers to leave the camp swiftly in any direction. The main exit faced away from the enemy and was called the ***porta decumana*** (because the tenth cohort camped near it). The ***porta praetoria*** was closest to the enemy and the commanding officer's quarters (***praetorium***). The ***via praetoria*** led from the *porta decumana* to the *praetorium*. The exits on the left- and right-hand sides were known as the ***porta principalis sinistra*** and ***porta principalis dextra***. The main road through the camp ran between these two exits and was called the ***via principalis***.

Camp buildings

The most important building in the camp was the *principia*, where the general and his staff had their headquarters. The *principia* was placed at the crossroads of the two main roads. It was easy to find and the officers could oversee all the comings and goings of the camp. The eagles were kept in part of the *principia* known as the *sacellum*. Money was stored in the treasury (which was often underground for safety), although pay was given out from the paymaster's quarters (*quaestorium*). The *augurale*, or altar for the augurs to take omens, was also nearby. Soldiers paraded either in the *basilica* – a large hall attached to the *principia* – or in a parade ground outside the camp. Officers addressed their men from the speaker's platform (*tribunal*).

Large permanent camps had bath-houses (*thermae*) where the soldiers could relax and get clean. These were often outside the camp walls in case the furnaces caused a fire. Camps also contained hospitals, with surgeons and medical assistants, and granaries to store food supplies. In a permanent camp, the commanding officer's living quarters were often in a house where he and his family lived. Officers had quarters in the *praetorium* or, in large camps, in houses of their own. Soldiers slept either in barracks or in leather tents. Centurions slept in larger tents or rooms in the barracks. At least a thirty-metre gap was left between tents or barracks and the rampart. This gap was known as the *intervallum* and ensured that the tents were out of range of enemy missiles.

Settlements (*vici*) often sprang up outside the camps as merchants came to sell their wares (particularly food and wine). As the soldiers got to know the locals, many ended up with girlfriends. Until 197 AD, soldiers of *optio* rank and below were not allowed to marry, but many had long-term partners and families living outside the camp. These relationships were generally made legal when a soldier was discharged from his legion.

It was essential to maintain a close guard over the camp in case of unexpected attack. Guards (*custodes*) were posted on the walls, at the gates and on the ramparts. Some guards were also based in outposts (*stationes*) to give early warning of any attack. Guard duty was taken very seriously and any soldier who fell asleep on duty was severely punished. Sleeping on duty was a particular danger during the four night watches (*vigiliae*), each of which lasted around three hours.

9.4 Tombstones

One important source of evidence about the Roman army comes from tombstones. Roman tombstones often contain information about where a soldier had served and with which legion. Some tombstones also have carvings depicting soldiers in uniform – these carvings provide useful additional evidence to written descriptions of military life. For example, a tombstone with a carving of an *aquilifer* holding his eagle gives us a contemporary representation of an eagle, as well as confirming that the dead soldier or his family wanted to record that he had reached this rank. Similarly, tombstones that preserve the campaign honours won by a soldier indicate which legions were in action at certain times. Other tombstones may record who set them up, giving details of wives, freedmen and friends.

Roman tombstones followed certain conventions. In particular, many inscriptions use abbreviations. This meant that more information could be fitted onto the stone, although it does make them harder to read. The first line of the tombstone normally included *D. M.*, which stood for *Dis Manibus* and meant 'to the spirits of the dead'. The next piece of information was the name of the dead man. Roman citizens had three names, the **praenomen** (or first name), **nomen** (clan name) and **cognomen** (family name). These were all listed on the tombstone, although the *praenomen* was normally abbreviated. For example, *M.* stood for Marcus (see below for other abbreviations). The *nomen* and the *cognomen* were given in full. Gravestones also often recorded the abbreviated form of the father's *praenomen*, often followed by *F.* for *filius*. For example, *Q. F.* stood for *Quinti filius* – the son of Quintus. Sometimes we can tell from non-Roman names that the dead person was originally a foreigner who had been granted Roman citizenship. For example, Tiberius Claudius Cogidubnus, king of the region near Chichester, has the very non-Roman *cognomen* of Cogidubnus.

The tombstone of a cavalry officer who was stationed at Scarbantia

Abbreviations of Roman names:

A. = Aulus   C. = Gaius   Cn. = Gnaeus   D. = Decimus   L. = Lucius
M. = Marcus   P. = Publius   Q. = Quintus   S. = Sextus   Ser. = Servius
Sp. = Spurius   T. = Titus   Ti. = Tiberius

In addition, each Roman citizen belonged to one of the thirty-five Roman tribes. As the names of the tribes were well known, they were often abbreviated on tombstones. For example, VOL stood for Voltini. Roman tombstones normally gave the dead man's *praenomen* and *nomen* before recording who his father was. Then the dead man's tribe was noted and finally his *cognomen*. Many tombstones also recorded the birthplace of the dead man.

Men who had served in the legions recorded their rank and legion. Much of this information was also normally abbreviated. For example, *OPT LEG II AUG* stood for *optio legionis II Augustae* (*optio* of the Second Legion, the Augusta). *VET* stood for *Veteranus* (veteran), and the sign > showed that the dead man had been a centurion. Some tombstones also recorded a man's length of service in the legions. This was written as *STP* or *STIP* followed by a number. Thus *STIP XIV* stood for *stipendia* or *stipendiorum XIV* (fourteen years' service). A man's age at time of death was marked by *AN* or *ANN* followed by a number. *AN* stood for *annos* or *annorum* (years). Some tombstones also included the abbreviation *VIX*, which stood for *vixit* (he lived).

At the end of the inscription it was common to write *HSE* or *HFC*. These stood for *hic situs est* (here is buried) and *heres faciendum curavit* (his heir set this up).

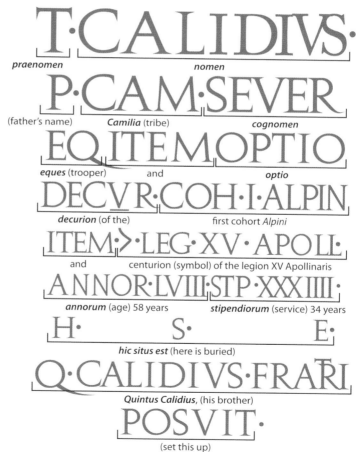

The tombstone for Titus Calidius Severus, son of Publius, recording his life and military service

Exercise 9.1

1. (a) Draw a detailed plan of the command structure of the Roman army from the overall commander down to the *contubernia*.
   (b) State two benefits of this sort of command structure.
2. (a) Outline the variety of tasks undertaken by Roman soldiers, including specialists in the first cohort and various signal-bearers.
   (b) Which role would you have most liked to have had in the Roman Army and why?
3. (a) Explain in detail what sort of tasks non-citizens who served in the Roman army might undertake and how they were commanded.
   (b) Why do you think that so many non-Roman men chose to join the Roman army?

Extension work

You are a recruiting officer for the Roman army. Make a speech to your class setting out the conditions of service, what sort of roles are available and the benefits on offer to those who join. You may want to carry out further research into the sort of trades the Romans preferred to recruit from and those they did not.

Exercise 9.2

1. (a) Describe the various offensive weapons and equipment that Roman soldiers and auxiliaries carried.
   (b) What do you think was the most important item of equipment that was issued to Roman soldiers? Explain why you think this.
2. (a) Describe the defensive equipment available to Roman troops and what this equipment was made from.
   (b) Explain whether you think the *testudo* was a successful formation and why.
3. (a) Explain what sort of animals and machines were used in the Roman army and what they were used for.
   (b) What machine do you think would have been most effective and why?

Extension work

You are writing the obituary of a Roman military engineer. Write the section that deals with his views on equipment and machines. Remember that you need to include lots of accurate, historical detail – do not merely describe violent battles.

Exercise 9.3

1. (a) Draw a detailed diagram of a typical Roman army camp and label as many features as possible in both Latin and English.
   (b) Why do you think Roman army camps were built to a standard plan?

2. (a) Describe how a Roman army camp was constructed. Refer to the various
defensive elements, the layout and the tools used in the process.
   (b) Why do you think that most Roman soldiers preferred to be based in a
permanent camp rather than a temporary camp? Give two reasons for your
answer.

3. (a) Describe the buildings you would see if you were to walk round a permanent
Roman army camp – refer to buildings inside and outside the camp. Use
Latin names wherever possible.
   (b) Name two similarities OR dissimilarities between Roman army camps and
modern army camps.

Extension work

Make a model of a Roman army camp in as much detail as possible. Label the
features in Latin and English.

Exercise 9.4

1. (a) Describe what sort of abbreviations are used on the tombstones of Roman
soldiers.
   (b) Give examples of two important differences between Roman tombstones and
modern tombstones.

2. (a) Draw a diagram of a typical Roman tombstone, label the various sections
and explain what they mean (for example, heading, name, tribe, etc.).
   (b) Why do you think that some Romans chose to include this level of detail on
their tombstones?

3. (a) As well as information about the dead soldier, archaeologists can often gain
further information from tombstones about other people or the Roman army
in general. Explain what this information is.
   What information can you work out from the following inscription?
   > LEG II AUG
   STP XVI
   VIX ANN XXXV
   (b) Give one reason why someone might want to have a carving on his
tombstone and one reason why a carving might not be included.

Extension work

Research further examples of Roman army tombstones. Write an essay or
presentation assessing the value of tombstones as a source of evidence about life in
the Roman Army. What other forms of evidence are available and how reliable are
they?

CHAPTER 10 ROMAN BRITAIN

10.1 Julius Caesar in Britain

Julius Caesar was probably the most famous Roman ever, but he is particularly important to the history of Britain because he invaded the country in 55 BC. The Romans had been aware of the existence of Britain for many years before they invaded. British goods made their way to Gaul and the Romans knew that Britain produced tin, iron, silver, gold, timber and hunting dogs. Britain was situated far away from Rome and, as such, was one of the last provinces to be added to the Roman Empire. Britain also had a certain glamour attached to it because little was known about the region.

At this time, Britain was not a united island. Instead, different regions were inhabited by different tribes, each ruled by its own king. For example, the Iceni were based in what is now Norfolk, the Catuvellauni ruled Hertfordshire and the Durotriges controlled Dorset and Wiltshire. The Atrebates were strong in Hampshire and Berkshire, while the Brigantes were the most important tribe in the north of England. Wales was occupied by the Deceangli, Ordovices, Demetae and Silures. Various tribes throughout Scotland were known to the Romans as the Caledonii, but the Picti (Picts or Painted People), who inhabited the far north of Scotland, did not come to Roman attention for some time.

The first Roman general to show a real interest in Britain was Julius Caesar. Gaius Julius Caesar was born in 102 BC into a patrician family of great nobility. He was very proud of his ancestors and was determined to be an outstanding politician. He joined the army with the intention of making a name for himself and he proved to be a brilliant general, loved and respected by his men.

Caesar was a superb tactician and was ruthless in his pursuit of military glory. He conquered much of Gaul (modern France and Belgium) and gained considerable wealth from selling captured Gauls as slaves. However, Caesar was not content to remain in Gaul – he needed more fame to strengthen his bid for political power – nor could he risk giving up his military command and leaving his army to be taken over by his political rivals. Thus Britain was Caesar's next objective. Very little was known about the island and anyone who crossed the 'Ocean' to Britain would gain great glory in Rome. Moreover, the island was reputed to be wealthy, particularly in terms of metals (tin, gold and silver) and Caesar could expect to enslave many newly conquered tribesmen.

Caesar lost little time in coming up with a good excuse for the invasion of Britain: he claimed that British tribesmen had been supplying aid to rebellious tribes in Gaul. In 55 BC he gathered a small force of two legions and set off on an exploratory mission. As the ships drew up to the landing places on the beaches in Kent, the soldiers were loath to disembark. Petrifying tales had spread round the legionaries about the unknown island that they were about to invade. It was a land of mists and terrifying warriors, who were reputed to paint themselves blue with woad (a dye derived from a native plant). The British even had priests called druids who sacrificed humans! However, the *aquilifer* (or standard-bearer) of Legio X was disgusted with his comrades' cowardice. Seizing his eagle, he leapt out of the ship onto the sands. To lose an eagle to the enemy was a dreadful disgrace and the other legionaries felt compelled to follow their *aquilifer*. The British forces were defeated.

Although Caesar had established a landing place, he was not able to do much more than carry out a reconnaissance mission, partly because his ships were damaged in a

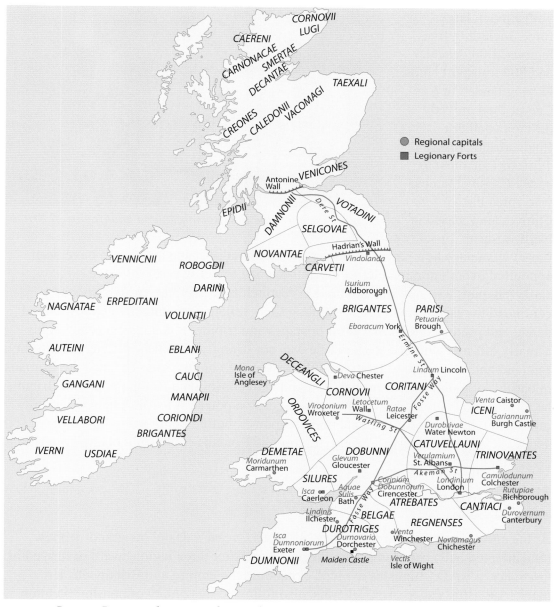

Roman Britain, showing tribes and towns, as well as the main Roman roads
(Sources: *Ordnance Survey Map of Roman Britain* and *An Imperial Possession* by David Mattingly)

storm and partly because it was the end of the campaigning season when the increasing cold and harsh wintry weather made fighting very difficult. The next year (54 BC), he returned with a much larger force, including five legions, 2,000 cavalry and 800 transport ships. Having landed in Kent, Caesar then moved through southern England and crossed the Tamesis (Thames) to attack Cassivellaunus, who ruled the Catuvellauni, based in Hertfordshire.

Julius Caesar – the first Roman to lead an invasion of Britain

Cassivellaunus was a powerful player in British politics and appears to have been appointed overall commander of the anti-Roman forces. Caesar defeated Cassivellaunus's troops and captured his capital. However, the British troops continued to resist Roman rule. Although Cassivellaunus eventually acknowledged defeat and promised to give Caesar hostages and tribute, it is not clear whether he actually did so. Certainly, Roman rule was not strongly established. Only south-east England had submitted to Rome and the rest of the country had not faced the Romans in battle. Although Caesar probably intended to consolidate Roman power in Britain, he returned to Gaul after a few months to quash a potential revolt. Then he became involved in his quest for ultimate political power, before being assassinated in 44 BC. It would be nearly a century before the Romans could truly claim Britain as one of their provinces.

10.2 Claudius

At the end of the civil war that followed Julius Caesar's death, his grand-nephew (and adopted heir), Augustus, became emperor. After three legions were destroyed in Germany in 9 AD, Augustus avoided expanding the empire and Britain was left alone. Augustus's successor, Tiberius, also followed this policy of non-intervention. However, in 40 AD, the next emperor, Caligula, led an invasion force as far as

Gesoriacum (Boulogne), where it halted. Caligula ordered his troops to collect thousands of seashells, before claiming that the shells were the loot from his successful campaign. Whether Caligula really believed that he had conquered Britain is unclear – but no one else thought that he had. However, things were about to change under his successor, the Emperor Claudius.

Claudius was a highly intelligent man, but he suffered from physical disabilities. In a society that was very conscious of its military power and where most upper-class men served for several years in the army, some people despised Claudius as a weakling. Claudius knew this and he saw a successful invasion of Britain as an excellent means of gaining military glory for himself. Moreover, Claudius had come to power following the murder of Caligula and he needed to prove himself as a successful ruler.

Claudius could claim that, during the time of Caesar's invasion of Britain, at least some of the British tribes had acknowledged Rome as their overlord. Also, many British tribes feared the growing power of the Catuvellauni and were, therefore, happy to ask the Romans to protect them. Although the Catuvellauni were historically based in Hertfordshire, their king Cunobelinus (immortalised by Shakespeare as Cymbeline) had expanded their power base considerably. Cunobelinus had conquered the Trinovantes of Essex and, when Cunobelinus died in 40 AD, his sons Caratacus and Togodumnus had no intention of abandoning their father's conquests. The Catuvellauni posed no threat to Roman rule in Gaul, but the possibilities of loot and military glory attracted Claudius and he soon organised a strong invasion force, led by Aulus Plautius.

At first, the troops refused to embark on a journey outside the known world. However, in 43 AD, Plautius led four legions (II Augusta, IX Hispana, XIV Gemina and XX Valeria Victrix), backed up by auxiliary forces, across the Channel. As many as 40,000 men were involved and the Romans made an unopposed landing at **Rutupiae (**Richborough) in Kent. The Romans swiftly defeated Caratacus on the Medway and crossed the Thames. Caratacus now fell back to **Camulodunum** (Colchester) and there was a delay while the emperor Claudius crossed from Gaul. Claudius brought war elephants with him, but he only stayed in Britain for sixteen days until Camulodunum fell. Claudius then returned to Rome to celebrate a triumph.

Although the Romans had captured Camulodunum, they still had to pacify the rest of the country. One legionary commander, Vespasian (who was to become emperor in 69 AD), was sent to mop up the tribes on the south coast. Vespasian faced fierce fighting, particularly since he had to capture twenty hill forts. Sieges could take months while the defenders were starved out, so Vespasian decided to take them by force, using siege machines, such as *catapultae* or *ballistae*. The important and well-defended hill fort of Maiden Castle near **Durnovaria** (Dorchester) was attacked by Legio II Augusta in 43 AD and the siege machines worked – a skeleton of one of the defenders has been found with a *ballista* bolt lodged in his vertebrae. After sustained fighting, Vespasian conquered the Durotriges and another southern tribe (possibly the Dumnonii of Devon). Other legions were helping to suppress central England and by 47 or 48 AD the conquered territory reached along the Fosse Way from **Isca Dumnoniorum** (Exeter) in the south to **Lindum** (Lincoln) in the north.

In some areas, the Romans set up 'client kingdoms' where a local king ruled the region but was also loyal to Rome. Such a system meant that the Romans could claim that the native British were ruled by their own leaders,

Maiden Castle was an impressive Iron Age fort near Dorchester which the general Vespasian captured using siege machines

while still ensuring that taxes were collected and that external politics were firmly under Roman control. For example, Cogidubnus, who ruled much of the south of England based at his capital in Chichester, was made a Roman citizen and given a proper Roman name – Tiberius Claudius Cogidubnus. However, not every British leader wanted to co-operate.

10.3 Caratacus and Boudicca

Caratacus

While Claudius's invasion of Britain (43 AD) had started very successfully, large parts of the country remained unconquered. In particular, Caratacus, the king of the Catuvellauni, posed a considerable threat. Caratacus hated the Romans and longed for his people to be free. He had fought bravely to defend Camulodunum (Colchester), but when the town fell, Caratacus fled westwards into Wales. He continued to stir up resistance against the Romans and many tribesmen were spurred on to rebellion by his example.

The new overall commander of the Roman forces, Ostorius Scapula, was determined to capture Caratacus and put an end to his threat to Roman rule. Ostorius had already fought against the Deceangli in North Wales and now Caratacus was stirring up the Silures in South Wales and the Ordovices in central Wales. The Romans marched against Caratacus and defeated his forces near the River Severn. Caratacus fled to the Brigantes in northern England (Yorkshire and Lancashire). The queen of the Brigantes, Cartimandua, handed Caratacus over to the Romans. Cartimandua probably acted from political reasons. Her kingdom was wracked with political disagreements and she may have hoped that the Romans would help her to maintain power. However, it is likely that many tribesmen regarded her as a traitor.

Caratacus was sent to Rome as a captive and forced to march in chains through Rome as part of a triumph. Although being treated like a slave must have been humiliating for the proud king, he refused to show any fear, even though he knew that Claudius intended to put him to death at the end of the ceremony. However, Claudius was so impressed by Caratacus's bravery and nobility that he refused to kill him, preferring to keep him and his family as honoured guests in Rome.

Boudicca

For ten years after the defeat of Caratacus, the Romans were busy campaigning in Wales. However, in 60–61 AD, the Romans nearly lost control of Britain. When Prasutagus, the king of the East Anglian Iceni died, his will named his two daughters and the Roman Emperor, Nero, as his heirs. However, the Romans seized his entire kingdom, treating the Iceni as a defeated people. When Prasutagus's widow, Boudicca, protested, the local Romans flogged her and raped her daughters. Boudicca burned for revenge, as did the Iceni, who deeply resented this insult to their royal family. The Iceni had revolted in 47 AD when the Romans tried to disarm them and they did not trust the Romans. Their neighbours, the Trinovantes, had been expelled from Camulodunum (Colchester) to make way for Roman veteran soldiers and the Iceni feared that they would be next. They had also been paying heavy taxes to the Romans and many owed large sums to Roman money-lenders. The Romans now chose to call in their loans. When Boudicca called upon her people, they rose up, joined by the Trinovantes.

This fine bronze statue of Boudicca, sited near the Houses of Parliament, was commissioned by Prince Albert, the husband of Queen Victoria

At this point, in 60 AD, the governor of Britain, Suetonius Paulinus, was attempting to kill the last of the Druids and to destroy their sacred groves of trees on **Mona** (Anglesey). The Druids supported rebellions against the Romans and, in any case, the Romans thought that the Druids were uncivilized barbarians – particularly because they practised human sacrifice. While Paulinus was clearly carrying out a useful task for the Romans, it was unfortunate that he was far away when the Iceni and the Trinovantes swept through southern England.

Boudicca's first move was to burn Camulodunum (Colchester), slaughtering all the Roman inhabitants she could catch. Quintus Petillius Cerialis led a detachment of Legio IX from Lindum (Lincoln), but was driven back with heavy losses. This humiliating defeat helped Boudicca recruit more Britons to her army and she now led her troops against **Londinium** (London) and **Verulamium** (St Albans). The commander of Legio II Augusta refused to come to their aid and, although Suetonius Paulinus had returned from Wales with his cavalry, his infantry had not yet arrived. Both towns were sacked and burned to the ground. Roman settlers and pro-Roman Britons perished in great numbers (around 70,000 according to ancient sources) and the survivors were terrified that the whole region would fall to Boudicca.

Boudicca now made a major error by allowing Paulinus to fight on his choice of ground. The site of the battle is unknown, but although the Romans were outnumbered by around ten to one, their superior training and discipline enabled them to beat Boudicca's enormous force of up to 100,000 men. Many of the tribesmen's families had come to watch their men defeat the Romans. Instead, when the Britons turned to flee, their escape route was hindered by non-combatants clogging up the fields. The Romans slaughtered whoever they could lay their hands on: it is estimated that around 80,000 Britons were killed. Thousands were enslaved and Boudicca committed suicide. Boudicca had been charismatic and determined to defeat the Romans; without such a strong, committed leader the rebellion soon died out. The Romans consolidated their hold on Britain, Paulinus was recalled and new governors pushed Roman rule further north.

10.4 Towns in Britain

Roman towns grew up throughout Britain. Sometimes they took the place of an existing British settlement, while others were created by the Romans. First, a suitable site was chosen with level land, a reliable water supply and good communications, such as rivers or existing roads. For example, Londinium had excellent communications along the River Thames and became a busy port, importing goods (such as olive oil or wine) from across the Empire.

Some Roman towns were *coloniae*. These were settlements that were built to house retired legionaries and their families. There were four *coloniae* in Britain. The first was built in 49 AD on the site of the captured tribal capital of Camulodunum.

Lindum was founded in the 80s or 90s AD and **Glevum** (Gloucester) was built between 96 and 98 AD. **Eboracum** (York) was a garrison town, which was given the status of a *colonia* in the early 200s.

Many settlements grew up near Roman army camps and, if you live in a town that has –chester or –cester as part of its name, then you probably live somewhere that used to have a Roman camp (*castra*). For example, Chester was the site of a large legionary camp (called **Deva**) and Cirencester (**Corinium Dobunnorum**) still preserves many important Roman remains.

Roman towns normally had a regular layout, based on a grid plan. Streets ran in straight lines and the centre of any town was the forum. Citizens often gathered here to take part in elections or to hear important announcements from the ***rostrum*** (speaker's platform). The forum normally contained a temple and at one end of the forum was the ***basilica*** – a long hall with a colonnade of columns. Many activities took place in the *basilica*. The town treasury was kept there and the *basilica* also housed the headquarters of the imperial cult, where sacrifices were made for the safety of the emperor. The ***tribunal*** was part of the *basilica* where law courts met to hear cases and council meetings were held in another section, called the ***curia***.

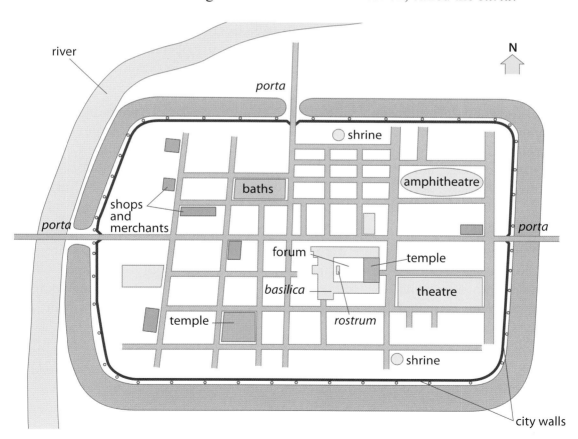

Although not every Roman town would have a river nearby, surveyors would look for a good water supply before they selected a site for a town

Roman towns contained many shops. Goldsmiths, glass merchants, jewellers, blacksmiths, leather workers, textile workers and slave dealers might be found in larger towns, while most towns would have bakers, butchers, vegetable sellers, cobblers and potters, as well as bars selling drink and snacks.

Towns were run by a town council, which was supposed to consist of one hundred decurions (wealthy men over the age of thirty), who elected two senior magistrates and two junior magistrates. Many men preferred not to become decurions, as councillors were expected to pay for improvements to the town! However, important local men sometimes set up public monuments. For example, there were at least three triumphal arches in Verulamium (St Albans). Some towns also built walls. Remains of such city walls still exist in Chester, York and London.

Archaeological excavations have revealed much about Roman towns. We know that towns had proper water supplies (including drains). Although the British climate meant that aqueducts were less frequently built than in Italy, they were sometimes used to supply the public baths. For example, an aqueduct provided the water pressure needed to supply the public baths in Lindum (Lincoln). Bathing was a key part of Roman daily life as people enjoyed socialising in informal surroundings. Bath complexes were found in most Roman towns and varied in size according to the wealth of the city. Some places, such as Aquae Sulis (Bath), were known for their healing properties and attracted many visitors. In the case of Bath, the Romans continued a pre-Roman tradition of the healing springs – Sulis was the local Celtic goddess.

Other forms of entertainment were available. Theatres appear to have been less popular than baths, but the theatre in **Durovernum** (Canterbury) was large, with a capacity of 7,000. Amphitheatres hosted gladiatorial shows and beast hunts, as well as public meetings, military training, parades and the execution of criminals. Eight amphitheatres have been found so far in Britain, including at Chester. Race tracks were also sometimes available (as at Colchester), although these are difficult to trace archaeologically.

Throughout Roman Britain there were large numbers of temples, from magnificent buildings in major cities to small shrines on Hadrian's Wall. Both Roman and Celtic gods were worshipped and the Romans introduced many gods to Britain, including Mithras, who represented the battle between good and evil and was popular with soldiers.

A vital method of communication between towns was Roman roads, which travelled straight through natural obstacles, such as marshes. Several important modern roads still follow a route first used by the Romans. Roman roads were well built, with a cambered, raised surface so that water drained off into ditches at the side and did not flood the road. These roads, such as the Fosse Way, Akeman Street and Watling Street, opened Britain up to travellers. It was now possible to travel quickly and in relative safety, while the military authorities could move troops swiftly to the site of any trouble. Trade was also helped, particularly the transportation of the enormous quantities of supplies and food needed by army garrisons.

10.5 Villas

Romans imported new forms of housing into Britain. Houses in towns tended to be organised into blocks known as *insulae*. This was particularly common if the town was based on a decommissioned army camp. In the countryside, most people continued to live in the traditional British round-house, but wealthier Roman settlers and native British landowners built *villae*. Villas were constructed from stone with timber upper storeys and they varied in size from small farmhouses to extensive country houses with large numbers of elegant rooms.

Many villas were designed to impress visitors. A splendid villa showed that the person who lived there was wealthy, influential and important. Therefore it made sense for important Romans to live in fine houses so that they might impress the local tribal chiefs with their power. Sometimes local tribesmen adopted a similar lifestyle. One possible example of this is the palace of Fishbourne, near Chichester. Although archaeologists are not certain that this magnificent building was created for a British chief, it is situated five kilometres away from the tribal capital of the Atrebates at **Noviomagus** (Chichester) and would have been a suitable base for the tribal ruler,

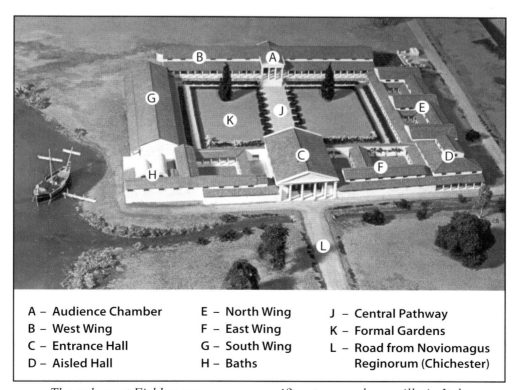

A – Audience Chamber	E – North Wing	J – Central Pathway
B – West Wing	F – East Wing	K – Formal Gardens
C – Entrance Hall	G – South Wing	L – Road from Noviomagus
D – Aisled Hall	H – Baths	Reginorum (Chichester)

The palace at Fishbourne was as magnificent as any large villa in Italy and was built by specialist craftsmen brought from Italy

Tiberius Claudius Cogidubnus (sometimes known as Togidubnus). Cogidubnus had been made a Roman citizen by the Emperor Claudius and was probably introduced to all the best things that the Romans had to offer, including villas.

Building at Fishbourne started around 75 AD. There was an assembly hall, a set of private baths, an audience chamber and other reception areas, all laid out around a formal garden. There were also many private rooms. The villa was lavishly decorated with carved stone columns and exceptional mosaics. Some walls were covered with slabs of marble, while others had painted frescoes (often of plants). The garden was created to a Roman design with trees, lawns, flower beds and fountains. This villa, built early in the Roman occupation, was as magnificent as any contemporary villa in Italy itself. The site occupies over four hectares of land and the architects of such a vast building would have come from Italy, as would most of the specialist craftsmen who worked there.

Although Fishbourne is one of the finest surviving Roman villas, there were numerous villas in Roman Britain. Many were built in the fourth century and the majority were attached to working farms. However, this did not mean that they were not luxurious. For example, the Roman villa of Bignor in Sussex was decorated with fine mosaics and had a set of private baths with an underfloor heating system (hypocaust). Similarly, the third-century villa at Chedworth in Gloucestershire had a large floor plan, with an impressive colonnade and fine mosaics. Large villas that were clearly run at a profit tend to be found in the south of England where there were many towns where produce could be sold. Villas in the north of England were less wealthy, partly because there were fewer towns nearby and also because the region was less settled than the south and was occupied by the army.

Although villas varied in size, most had a private bath-house and the living quarters were often heated by a hypocaust. The finest had glass windows and colonnaded walks for the owner and his guests to stroll through. The working part of the house would contain storage rooms for food and farm equipment, as well as the slaves' quarters. Rooms were decorated with painted plaster frescoes and mosaics. Rich villa owners would have had elegant furniture and expensive possessions, such as silver candelabra and jugs.

10.6 Hadrian's Wall

The Emperor Hadrian visited Britain in 122 AD as part of his tour of the Roman Empire. He decided that he wanted to stabilise the frontiers of the Roman world and ordered a wall to be built from the Solway Firth, near Carlisle, to the Tyne estuary at Newcastle. Hadrian's Wall was nearly 117 kilometres long and took around five years to build.

Most of the wall was built of stone and some turf ramparts in the western half were later replaced by stone walls. The wall was over six metres high and varied from two and a half to three metres thick. The wall had a parapet that soldiers could walk along and the ramparts were crenellated to give the soldiers protection as they looked out. Every Roman mile (1,481 metres) there was a small fort, known as a milecastle, and between each of the 80 milecastles there were two watch towers, or turrets. Turrets served as lookout posts and there was a turret or a milecastle every 494 metres. Turrets were built of stone, but milecastles in the western section were made of wood and turf. The numbers of men attached to each milecastle varied, with some holding as many as thirty-two and some as few as eight. The lookouts in the turrets were probably based at each milecastle and rotated duties.

The original plan had not included large forts on the wall itself, but things changed around 126 AD. At that point sixteen forts were built, spread along the wall. Each fort housed a cohort of 500 or 1,000 soldiers. Although the wall had been built by legionaries and was maintained by them, the troops stationed on the wall were auxiliaries – for example, Housesteads was home to 1,000 auxiliary troops.

Roman soldiers would have manned Hadrian's Wall in winter and summer

The wall was not the only protection from northern tribes. A deep ditch was dug on the northern side of the wall, except where the wall ran along high crags, making a ditch unnecessary. On the southern side of the wall was another deep ditch called the **vallum**. This was six metres wide and three metres deep with a two and a half metre flat gap along its bottom. Between the wall and the *vallum* there was a military road connecting the forts – soldiers could travel swiftly along this road. Since Cumbria was considered vulnerable to attack from sea raiders from what is now Scotland, there was a forty-two-kilometre extension of the milecastle and turret system down the western coast. Although there was no wall connecting these coastal forts, it is possible that there may have been a wooden palisade that ran between the various turrets.

Hadrian's Wall served several purposes. Although the Romans continued to hold land north of the Wall (in military outposts), the wall separated the restless tribes in Scotland and the north of England from the more settled lands further south. The wall also served as a long military base – soldiers could be quickly sent to trouble spots and the wall was a place from which to patrol and gather intelligence. Finally, the Wall also helped to control movement and to regulate trade – with a limited number of crossing points, all of which were manned, it was much easier to check that people were paying the correct dues and to halt any smuggling.

However, despite the clear benefits of Hadrian's Wall, another wall was built around 140 AD. The Antonine Wall was 130 kilometres further north than Hadrian's Wall and stretched from the Clyde to the Forth. It is unclear whether the new emperor, Antoninus Pius, ordered it to be built because he wanted to gain reflected glory from his new building project, or whether there were particular difficulties in the region. The Antonine Wall was sixty kilometres long and was built of turf. It had nineteen forts attached to it and, like Hadrian's Wall, the Antonine Wall had a deep ditch in front of it (at least three and a half metres deep and around twelve metres wide).

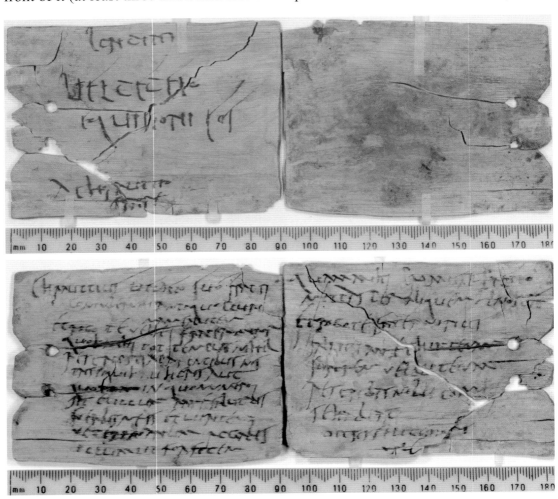

The Vindolanda tablets are written in ink on wood. This example shows the back (with address) and the front of a letter from Chrauttius to his former messmate, Veldeius, who was groom to the Governor in London

Around 6,000 or 7,000 men were based on the Antonine Wall, but the Romans withdrew to Hadrian's Wall in the mid to late second century AD.

One fort near Hadrian's Wall – **Vindolanda** – has enabled ordinary Romans to speak directly to us. Hundreds of writing tablets have been preserved in damp soil, giving us an unusual insight into life on the wall. In these tablets we learn of a soldier being sent underpants (*subligaria*) and socks (*udonum*) to keep him warm; an officer's wife delivers invitations to her birthday party and a schoolchild practises his writing. We also have records of different duties for soldiers at the fort (such as who was cleaning the latrines or mending kit). Those who were absent are noted as being off sick, out of the camp collecting pay or detached on guard duty.

10.7 Later rulers and the end of Roman Britain

In the 180s, tribes from unoccupied Britain began to raid areas controlled by the Romans. These raids were defeated, but Britain remained unsettled. In 193 AD, the governor of Britain, Clodius Albinus, declared himself Emperor. He was defeated in 197 in France by Septimius Severus. Severus took an active role in Britain. He campaigned from 208 to 211, marching into Scotland at least as far as the River Tay. Severus rebuilt much of Hadrian's Wall before he died in York in 211. Severus's elder son, Caracalla, wanted to secure his position as emperor and made peace with the tribes before withdrawing from Scotland. Roman Britain remained peaceful for nearly eighty years.

In 286 AD, Carausius, the commander of the Channel Fleet (based in Boulogne), was accused of keeping loot taken from pirates. He feared that he would be killed and fled to Britain, where he declared himself Emperor. Carausius was murdered in 293 AD by his treasurer, Allectus. The Emperor Constantius I defeated Allectus in 296 AD and brought Britain back into the wider Roman Empire. Constantius also defeated an invasion by the Picts in 306 AD, dying soon after. Constantius's son, Constantine the Great, was proclaimed Emperor at York.

Roman Britain was prosperous in the fourth century AD, as can be seen by the number of villas that were built at this time. However, raiders from the sea were becoming a problem and a series of forts was built on the south and east coasts (such as Burgh Castle in Norfolk). In 367–368 AD, Britain faced attacks by the Picts, Saxons and Scots (from Ireland), who were eventually defeated. However, barbarian attacks on the continent and civil war led to the withdrawal of badly needed troops. In 407 the last Roman troops were recalled and in 410 the inhabitants were told 'to look to their own defence'. By the late fifth century, Britain was in the hands of the Saxons. The great buildings and roads of the country slowly fell into disrepair – the new invaders lacked the skill to repair them and the Romano-British inhabitants were too concerned with staying alive. Roman Britain was at an end.

Exercise 10.1

1. (a) Outline the political situation in Britain and what the Romans knew about Britain before they invaded Britain in 55 BC. Why did Julius Caesar invade Britain?
   (b) Do you think Caesar was correct to invade Britain? Why?
2. (a) Describe the events of Caesar's invasion of 55 BC.
   (b) Do you believe Caesar's reason for invading Britain? Explain your answer.
3. (a) What happened when Caesar returned to Britain in 54 BC?
   (b) Overall, do you think that Caesar's claim to have conquered Britain is justified? Give reasons for your answer.

Extension work

Produce the front page of a newspaper reporting Caesar's invasion of Britain.

Exercise 10.2

1. (a) Outline the policy towards Britain of the first three Roman Emperors. Give details where possible.
   What political reasons had Claudius for invading Britain and what excuses did he give for the invasion?
   (b) Do you believe the reasons which were put forward for Claudius's invasion of Britain? Explain your answer.
2. (a) Outline the events of Claudius's invasion of Britain.
   (b) Do you think Claudius's invasion of Britain was more successful than that of Caesar? Why?
3. (a) You are serving in Legio II Augusta. Write an eye-witness account of your activities during the invasion and conquest of Britain.
   (b) After the invasion, the Romans set up client kingdoms. State one benefit and one danger to the Romans of doing this.

Extension work

Hold a class debate on why the Romans invaded Britain and whether you think Britain benefited from Roman rule.

Exercise 10.3

1. (a) Who was Caratacus? Why did he pose a threat to Roman rule and how was this threat dealt with?
   (b) If you had been Claudius, how would you have treated Caratacus? Give reasons for your answer.
2. (a) Explain why Boudicca's rebellion broke out and narrate the principal events of it.
   (b) Name two qualities that Boudicca displayed.

3. (a) Outline the main events of the rebellions of Caratacus and Boudicca.
   (b) Which do you think posed the greater threat to the Romans? Why?

Extension work

Produce a television news report on Boudicca. You may choose to focus on the outbreak of the revolt or the end of the revolt. Alternatively, divide your class into several groups and produce a regular news slot covering the entirety of the revolt. Remember to interview both British and Roman witnesses.

Exercise 10.4

1. (a) Draw a detailed plan of a typical Roman town. Include at least six features and label them (use Latin and English names wherever possible).
   (b) State two benefits of living in a Roman town.
2. (a) Explain how different types of Roman towns might have developed and explain what made a site especially suitable for a town. Describe what sort of activities took place in the forum.
   (b) Which activity would you most like to observe and why?
3. (a) Imagine that you live in Roman times. Describe a visit to your nearest town. Make sure that you describe the typical buildings that you might find.
   (b) Give two examples of aspects of modern towns that were not to be found in Roman towns.

Extension work

Write an illustrated guidebook for a visit to a Roman town as it would have appeared in Roman times (for example, Aquae Sulis or Verulamium). Include as many pictures and maps as possible.

Exercise 10.5

1. (a) Draw a diagram of a typical Roman villa, labelling as many features as possible in both Latin and English.
   (b) What benefits might the indigenous British have gained from the Roman occupation?
2. (a) Give a detailed description of the rooms, layout and decoration of villas in Roman Britain.
   (b) Name two negative aspects to the Roman occupation of Britain.
3. (a) Describe a visit to Fishbourne Palace in Roman times.
   (b) What do you think would have been the most impressive aspect of Fishbourne Palace and why do you think this?

Extension work

Research mosaics in villas from Roman Britain and then design a mosaic for a floor in your villa.

Exercise 10.6

1. (a) Describe the various elements that made up Hadrian's Wall.
   (b) Which do you think would be the most interesting section to serve on? Explain your answer.

2. (a) Give three purposes which Hadrian's Wall served and explain one of these in detail. Outline the history of the Antonine Wall.
   (b) Buildings are not the only things that have survived on Hadrian's Wall. Which document from Vindolanda do you think is the most interesting and why do you think this?

3. (a) Describe a typical day on patrol on Hadrian's Wall, making sure that you include as much detail about the wall as possible.
   (b) Give two reasons why soldiers might not have enjoyed being posted to Hadrian's Wall.

Extension work

Draw a plan of the wall and label it with detailed captions. Include the route taken by the wall, plus diagrams of a turret, milecastle and a fort.